Contents

Sensational Seasons: Summer, SV 9781419033940

Introduction

Preschool curriculum and instruction have been dramatically affected by the federal legislation that demands that schools *Put Reading First* and *No Child Is Left Behind* in achieving reading and math skills. Currently, the most important instructional focus in preschool classrooms is literacy development–providing environments in which young children can explore words, language, books, and print through developmentally appropriate literacy events.

In a literacy-rich classroom, children are surrounded with print, and their days are filled with activities that invite them to interact with print. Children are encouraged to "pretend" or attempt to read and write. Their attempts at reading and writing emergently are honored and valued as children move through the stages of development to become conventional readers and writers. So, the preschool teacher's role has changed from one of getting children "ready" to read to one of getting children reading and writing.

Activities Can Enrich Preschoolers' Literacy Experience

First Page of Each Unit Provides:

- Book List
- Teacher Information (Facts)

Second Page of Each Unit Provides:

- Illustrated Bulletin Board
- Materials List
- Teacher Preparation
- Student Directions

Third and Fourth Pages Provide Circle Time Lessons That Include:

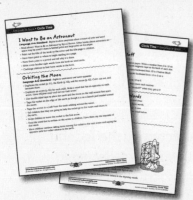

- Standard
- Language Arts, Math, and/or Science Skills
- Song or Poem

Fifth Page of Each Unit Provides:

- Standard
- Writing Activity
- Simple Snack Idea

Sixth and Seventh Pages Provide Center Ideas That Include:

- Standard
- Math Center Activity
- Language Center Activity
- Two Other Various Center Activities (Art, Science, and Sensory)

Remaining Pages of Each Unit Provide:

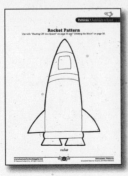

- Patterns and/or Activity Masters

Introduction
Sensational Seasons: Summer, SV 9781419033940

Standards

The following are preschool standards included with the activities and lessons in this book. Use these standards to guide further practice and to measure progress.

Language Arts	Page(s)
Begins to distinguish words in sentences	11, 85
Begins to recognize beginning sounds	11, 50
Begins to recognize high-frequency words	12, 30, 74
Organizes writing from left to right	13, 31, 88
Understands that letters make sounds	13, 66
Matches partner letters	14
Understands that reading progresses from left to right	20, 21, 48, 75
Makes illustrations to match words	22, 40
Recognizes rhyming words	23, 57, 77, 84
Shows awareness that different words begin with the same sound	29, 38, 66, 67
Demonstrates some ability to hear separate syllables in words	29, 47
Uses writing skills to convey meaning and information	32
Writes recognizable letters in own name	33
Communicates ideas and thoughts	30
Relates prior information to new information	38, 65
Listens effectively in informal situations	39
Actively participates in songs	39
Begins to understand alphabetical order	41
Communicates information with others	47
Identifies labels and signs in the environment	47
Uses scribbles, approximations of letters, or known letters to represent written language	49, 58
Begins to show awareness about concepts of print and word	56
Begins to understand and name opposites	56
Begins to identify onsets and rimes	57
Begins to recognize letters of the alphabet	59, 68
Writes to communicate for a variety of purposes	60, 86
Seeks answers to questions	74
Listens with understanding and responds to directions	74
Writes to produce numbers	76
Begins to name letters of the alphabet	84
Retells a story	84
Identifies letters in own name	87

Math	Page(s)
Counts objects using one-to-one correspondence	12, 48, 49, 59, 78
Describes and extends a pattern	14
Solves simple mathematical problems	21
Demonstrates a beginning understanding of measurement using non-standard units and measurement words	23, 68
Recognizes basic geometric shapes	32
Rote counts to 10	29, 75
Counts with understanding and recognizes "how many" in sets of objects	38
Uses concepts that include number recognition and counting	41, 85
Translates a pattern from one representation to another	50
Counts backward from 10 to 1	57
Begins to compare groups and recognize more than, less than, and equal to relationships	65
Fills a shape with solids or liquids	67
Recognizes and names numbers	77, 87

Science

Science	Page(s)
Displays curiosity about animals	15, 20, 24
Uses senses to observe and explore materials	31, 33, 42, 51, 58, 69
Begins to understand about scientific inquiry	60, 88

Social Studies

Social Studies	Page(s)
Begins to identify customs associated with national patriotic holidays	51

Art

Art	Page(s)
Explores a variety of techniques to create original work	15, 22, 24, 69, 76, 78, 86
Creates representations that contain increasing detail	42

Rhyming Picture Cards

The following cards may be used as a center activity, allowing children to match rhyming word cards, sort the cards into categories, or make up silly rhymes using the rhyming word pairs.

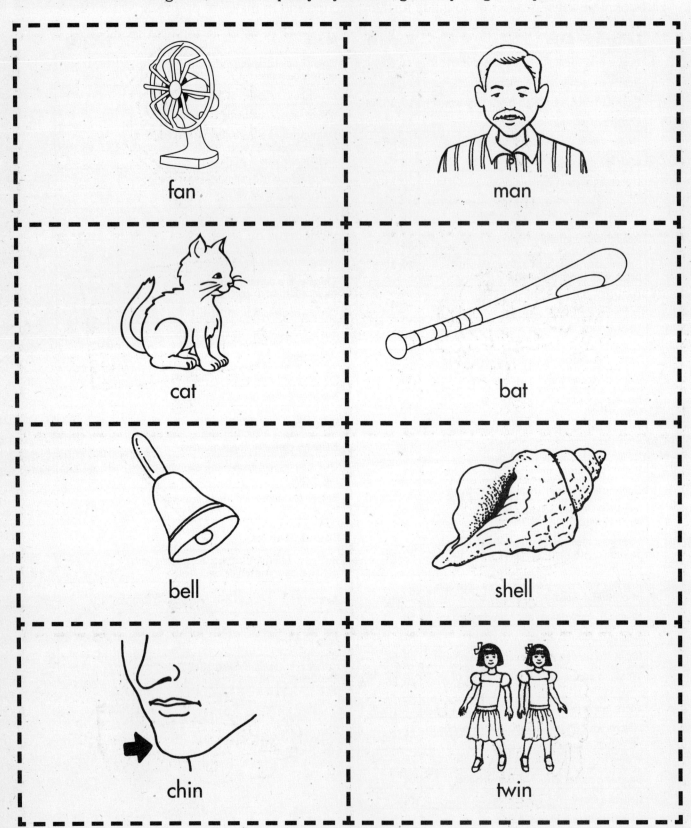

fan

man

cat

bat

bell

shell

chin

twin

Sensational Seasons: Summer, SV 9781419033940

Rhyming Picture Cards

mop

stop

bug

rug

cake

rake

sheep

jeep

Rhyming Picture Cards
Sensational Seasons: Summer, SV 9781419033940

Rhyming Picture Cards

boat

goat

moon

spoon

tie

pie

hose

nose

Rhyming Picture Cards

Sensational Seasons: Summer, SV 9781419033940

Books to Read

Ant Cities by Arthur Dorros (HarperTrophy)

Are You an Ant? by Judy Allen (Kingfisher)

Hey, Little Ant by Phillip M. Hoose (Tricycle Press)

I Can't, Said the Ant by Polly Cameron (Coward-McCann)

One Hundred Hungry Ants by Elinor J. Pinczes (Houghton Mifflin)

The Ant and the Elephant by Bill Peet (Houghton Mifflin)

The Little Red Ant and the Great Big Crumb by Shirley Climo (Clarion Books)

The Magic School Bus: Gets Ants in Its Pants by Joanna Cole (Scholastic Press)

Those Amazing Ants by Patricia Brennan Demuth (Simon & Schuster Children's Publishing)

Two Bad Ants by Chris Van Allsburg (Houghton Mifflin)

Ant Facts

Ants are common social insects that live in colonies with thousands of related ants. Each colony has a queen ant that begins her life with wings. She uses her wings to fly on a nuptial flight with male ants, during which she mates. The male ants will die soon afterward. The queen then flies to a nesting area, where she loses her wings and spends the rest of her life laying eggs. She takes care of the first eggs while they grow from larvae to pupae and then to adults. Most of the pupae will emerge as wingless female worker ants whose job will be collecting food for the colony members, defending the colony, and enlarging the colony. The female worker ants will also take care of the queen and her eggs. Some pupae will be smaller male ants that have wings and will fly from the colony to mate with a new queen. If the queen ant dies, the colony is able to survive only a few months.

Ants Underground

Materials

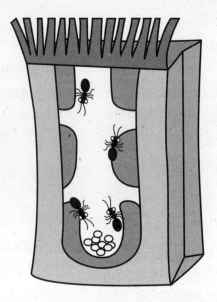

- ant tunnel pattern (p. 16)
- brown craft paper
- border
- brown lunch sacks
- green and black construction paper
- black beans and small white navy beans
- two small plastic bowls
- scissors
- glue
- stapler

Directions

Teacher Preparation: Duplicate the ant tunnel (p. 16) for use as a template. Trace the template on black construction paper and cut out one for each child. Cut two-inch by five-inch strips of green construction paper. Cut three inches off the top of each lunch sack so that it is about eight inches tall. Open the sack and cut a deep U-shape out of one side. Put the black and white beans in separate bowls. Cover the bulletin board with brown craft paper. Add a festive border and the caption.

1. Discuss with children how the ant colony is made up of different rooms or chambers. Some chambers, called nurseries, hold only the eggs laid by the queen.

2. Glue three black beans side by side to form the body of an ant on the black tunnel cutout. Repeat several times to make more ants.

3. Glue several white beans in one of the "chambers" as the eggs.

4. Glue the tunnel cutout on the inside of the lunch sack so that it is seen through the open side of the sack.

5. Use scissors to fringe the green paper strip to resemble grass.

6. Glue the grass across the top of the sack on the side that has been cut out.

7. Attach the "ant tunnels" by stapling the sacks to the bulletin board.

All About Ants

Language Arts Standard: *Begins to distinguish words in sentences*

- Use the ant (p. 17) as a model to draw several large ants about six inches long. Color, cut out, and laminate the ants.

- On the back of each one write an ant fact such as the ones below.

  Ants are insects that have six legs.
  Ants live in ant colonies with many other ants.
  Ant colonies have one queen ant that lays many eggs.

- Lay the ants across the floor as though they are walking on a trail.

- Invite children to pick up one ant. Turn the ant over and read the fact written on the back aloud to the children.

- On the board list key words from each fact, such as *insects*, *colonies*, and *queen*.

- Have children look at the sentences on the ants and find the key words.

Marching Ants

Language Arts Standard: *Begins to recognize beginning sounds*

- Cut out pictures of different kinds of food or use pieces of play food and put them inside a picnic basket.

- Use the ant (p. 17) as a model to draw large ants about six inches long. Color, cut out, and laminate the ants.

- Identify the letter of the beginning sound in the name of each type of food. Write the letters on the ants. Use the same ant for foods whose names begin with the same sound. For example, write *Cc* on one ant for foods such as *cake* and *cookie*.

- Place a picnic basket in the center of the rug in front of children. Lay the ants in a line as though they are walking away from the basket.

- Invite children to take out a "piece of food" from the basket and identify the letter that makes the beginning sound of the food name.

- Then have children lay the food next to the ant with the correct letter.

Food for the Queen

Math Standard: *Counts objects using one-to-one correspondence*

- Enlarge and duplicate ten picnic baskets (p. 17). Color them, cut along broken lines, and fold the lid back. Glue the baskets to construction paper, leaving the lid open. Trim the construction paper around the shape of the baskets.

- Place the picnic baskets on the floor around the classroom. Then put a generous supply of large lima beans in each basket. The lima beans will be the leftover "food crumbs."

- Tell children that you are the queen ant and they are the worker ants. Their job is to bring food to the queen.

- Have them sit on the rug around you. Then say a number. Have children "crawl" to a picnic basket and bring back the specified number of "food crumbs" to the queen.

- Continue naming numbers until the picnic baskets are empty.

In Tune with Language

Language Arts Standard: *Begins to recognize high-frequency words*

- Invite children to learn the following song, "The Ants Go Marching."

The ants go marching one by one,
Hurrah, hurrah.
The ants go marching one by one,
Hurrah, hurrah.
The ants go marching one by one.
The little one stops to suck his thumb.
And they all go marching down
Into the ground
To get out
Of the rain.
Boom, boom, boom, boom.

- Make cards with the numerals and number words for 1 to 10. Display them in a pocket chart.

- As the children sing, point to the card that corresponds to each verse in the song.

Ants in Your Pants

Language Arts Standard: *Organizes writing from left to right*

- Read children a book that has rhyming words, such as *I Can't, Said the Ant* by Polly Cameron.

- Discuss with them the meaning of the sentence *I have ants in my pants.* Have them identify the words that rhyme.

- Invite children to think of other silly sentences such as the ones below.

  I have blocks in my socks.
  I have fish in a dish.
  I have a frog on a log.

- Model writing the sentences on a chart and point out left to right progression. Hang the chart in view of the writing table.

- Encourage children to write their favorite sentence and illustrate it. Younger children may dictate the sentence or use scribble writing or letter-like forms.

Ants on a Log

Language Arts Standard: *Understands that letters make sounds*

- If possible, take children outside near a tree. Have them use a magnifying glass to look for ants crawling on the bark on the tree.

- Discuss with children what they see the ants doing. Tell them that they are going to have "ants" for a snack when they return to their classroom.

- Provide children with a three-inch piece of celery, a dab of softened cream cheese or peanut butter, and several raisins on a paper plate.

- Invite them to use a plastic knife to spread the cream cheese or peanut butter on the celery.

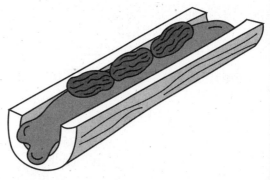

- Then have children press the raisins into the cream cheese or peanut butter to resemble ants on a log.

- Invite children to enjoy their snack.

- Challenge them to name the beginning, middle, and ending sounds of the word *ant.*

Caution: Be aware of children who may have food allergies.

Sensational Seasons: Summer, SV 9781419033940

Math Center

Math Standard:
Describes and extends
a pattern

Big Ant, Little Ant

- Discuss with children how patterns help us predict what comes next. Introduce them to simple ABABAB or AABAAB patterns.
- Duplicate 20 large ants and 20 small ants (p. 17). Color, cut out, and laminate them.
- Invite children to extend a simple pattern such as big ant, little ant, big ant, little ant.
- Challenge older children to make their own patterns and share them with a friend.

Language Center

Language Arts Standard:
Matches partner
letters

A Picnic Lunch

- Duplicate eight picnic baskets (p. 17). Cut along broken lines and fold the lid back. Glue the baskets to construction paper, leaving the lid open. Trim construction paper around the shape of the baskets.
- Write a target capital letter on the inside of each picnic basket.
- Enlarge and duplicate eight ants (p. 17). Color them brown and cut them out.
- Write the partner letters on each of the ants.
- Invite children to match the target and partner letters by putting the ants in the correct picnic baskets.

Art Center

Art Standard:
Explores a variety of techniques to create original work

It's Picnic Time

- Have children discuss a time when they went on a picnic. Have them tell if any ants came looking for food.

- Provide children with white construction paper, a two-inch square sponge, and red paint.

- Invite them to make a checkered tablecloth by using a sponge to paint red squares in rows across the white paper. Have them use a red, white, red, white pattern. Set aside to dry.

- Then have children press one finger on a black stamp pad and make three prints together to make the body of an ant on the tablecloth. Repeat the procedure to make as many ants as desired.

- Have children draw six legs and two antennae on each ant with a black fine-tipped marker.

- Encourage children to draw a picture of their favorite picnic food on a small paper plate. Have them glue the plate on their tablecloth next to the ants.

A Cool Drink of Water

Science Center

Science Standard:
Displays curiosity about animals

- Find an anthill and carefully scoop up enough of the anthill to fill a quart-sized jar about two-thirds full. Place a saturated cotton ball in the jar to provide water for the ants. Moisten the cotton ball daily. Cover the jar with a square of fabric and a rubber band. Place the jar in a brown paper bag to provide darkness for the ants.

- Read aloud a nonfiction book about ants from the book list (p. 9). Discuss with children the various jobs that worker ants do.

- Remove the jar from the bag and invite children to use a magnifying glass to see if the ants have begun making tunnels.

- Put food such as bread, cookie, or cracker crumbs in the jar daily. Have children predict which food the ants will eat first. Return the jar to the bag when it is not being observed.

- Invite children to write or dictate a sentence about what the ants are doing. Have them illustrate their sentence.

Ant Tunnel Pattern

Use with "Ants Underground" on page 10.

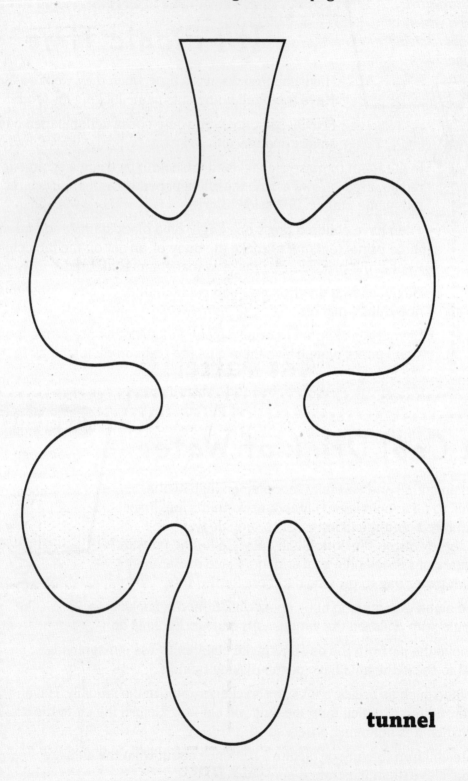

tunnel

Picnic Basket Pattern

Use with "Food for the Queen" on page 12 and "A Picnic Lunch" on page 14.

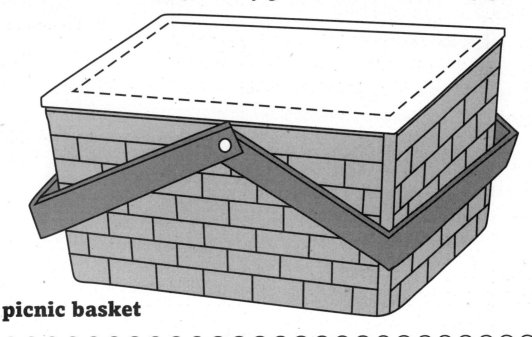

picnic basket

Ant Patterns

Use with "All About Ants" and "Marching Ants" on page 11,
and "Big Ant, Little Ant" and "A Picnic Lunch" on page 14.

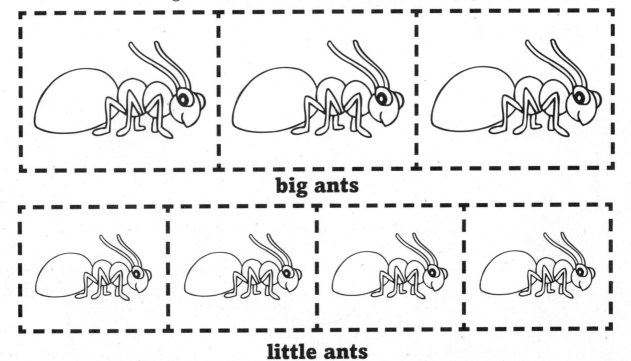

big ants

little ants

Ants: Patterns
Sensational Seasons: Summer, SV 9781419033940

Books to Read

Mister Seahorse by Eric Carle (Philomel)

One Lonely Sea Horse by Joost Elffers and Saxton Freymann (Arthur A. Levine Books)

Seahorses by Sylvia M. James (Mondo Publishing)

Seahorses by Twig C. George (Milbrook Press)

Seahorses and Sea Dragons by Mary Jo Rhodes (Children's Press)

Sea Horse: The Shyest Fish in the Sea by Chris Butterworth (Candlewick)

Secret Seahorse by Stella Blackstone (Barefoot Books)

Stevie B. Sea Horse: A Tale of a Proud Papa by Suzanne Tate (Nags Head Art, Inc.)

The Life Cycle of a Sea Horse by Bobbie Kalman (Crabtree Publishing Company)

Sea Horse Facts

The sea horse is a fish although it does not resemble one. It has a horse-like head and a monkey tail. The body of the sea horse is covered with rigid scales that look as though they are fused together. A sea horse's eyes move independently of each other. The height of a full-grown sea horse varies from 1½ inches to 14 inches. Sea horses vary in color, including orange, red, yellow, and green. However, they can change color to blend in with the surroundings. Sea horses live among seaweed, where they feed on plankton. When resting, sea horses attach themselves to coral or seaweed by their tail to keep from floating away. A female sea horse lays her eggs in a pouch on the male's stomach. In 2 to 6 weeks, the eggs develop into fully formed, miniature sea horses. Sea horses mate for life and like to swim in pairs linked by their tails.

Sensational Seasons: Summer, SV 9781419033940

See the Sea Horses

Materials

- blue craft paper
- border
- completed sea horses from "Torn Paper Sea Horses" on page 24
- green crepe paper
- scissors
- stapler

Directions

1. Cover the bulletin board with blue craft paper.

2. Cut various lengths of green crepe paper to make streamers.

3. Start at the bottom edge of the bulletin board and staple the streamers to the board to resemble seaweed. Slightly twist each piece to give it a three-dimensional effect.

4. Add a border and the caption.

5. Using the sea horses that children complete in "Torn Paper Sea Horses" on page 24, staple them to the bulletin board. Arrange them so that the tails are curled around the seaweed.

Sea Begins with S, and Horse Begins with H

Language Arts Standard: *Understands that reading progresses from left to right*

- Duplicate for each child a set of letters that spell *sea horse* (p. 26). Cut a four-inch by twelve-inch strip of construction paper for each child.

- Put a plastic or a real sea horse or a picture of a sea horse in a bag.

- Set the bag in front of children and invite them to guess what is in the bag. Give them the following clues.

  I live in the ocean. I am an unusual fish. I have a head like a horse. I have a tail like a monkey.

- Show children the sea horse and write *sea horse* on the board. Have children name the beginning sound of each word, count the number of letters in each word, and identify letters that are duplicated in both words.

- Provide each child with a set of letters, a strip of construction paper, scissors, and glue.

- Have children cut apart the letters in *sea horse*. Have them look at the two words on the board and glue the letters on the strip of paper in the correct sequence.

- Challenge them to name the letters in both words.

Daddy Sea Horse

Science Standard: *Displays curiosity about animals*

- Duplicate the sea horse and pouch (p. 25) for use as a template. Trace and cut out a daddy and mommy sea horse on felt. Use a marker to draw eyes.

- Trace and cut out two pouches from felt that match the color of the daddy sea horse. Stitch or hot glue a pouch to both sides of the daddy sea horse. Attach the pouches around the edges, leaving the top side open.

- Have several half-inch beads available to use as the eggs.

- Cut a pipe cleaner into one-inch pieces. Bend both ends of the pieces to form an S-shape. These will be the baby sea horses. Out of sight of children, put the babies into the pouch that is empty.

- Place the two sea horses facing each other on a flannel board. Have the pouch side that is empty facing up.

- Invite children to sing the song on page 21.

- During the first verse, stuff the "beads" into the pouch to resemble the mother laying the eggs in the daddy's pouch.

- During the second verse, turn the daddy sea horse over and pull the "babies" out of the pouch. Stick them to the flannel board.

- During the last verse, move the babies around the flannel board as though they are swimming around.

Baby Sea Horse Word Problems

Math Standard: *Solves simple mathematical problems*

• Make baby sea horses by cutting pipe cleaners into one-inch pieces. Bend the ends of each piece to form an S-shape.

• Provide each child with eight to ten "baby sea horses" and a half sheet of blue construction paper to use as a counting board.

• Invite children to count the correct number of sea horses on their counting board to solve the following word problems.

There were 3 baby sea horses. Then 1 more baby sea horse swam to them. How many baby sea horses were there altogether?

There were 4 baby sea horses looking for food. Two more babies joined them. How many baby sea horses were looking for food?

There were 6 baby sea horses playing one day. Then 2 babies swam away. How many baby sea horses were left?

• Continue with other word problems as long as children are interested.

In Tune with Language

Language Arts Standard: *Understands that reading progresses from left to right*

• Write the words to the following song on a chart.

• Have children learn the song to the tune of "London Bridge Is Falling Down." Invite them to follow along as you point to the words in the song.

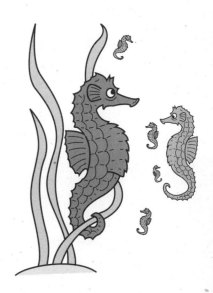

Mommy sea horse lays the eggs, lays the eggs, lays the eggs, Mommy sea horse lays the eggs in the daddy's pouch.

The babies grow in Daddy's pouch, Daddy's pouch, Daddy's pouch, The babies grow in Daddy's pouch, and then they hatch out.

Now the babies swim around, swim around, swim around, Now the babies swim around close to Mom and Dad.

Places I Like

Language Arts Standard: *Makes illustrations to match words*

- Have children pretend that a sea horse comes to visit them. It wants to visit their favorite place in their town or city.

- Encourage children to name a store, a restaurant, a park, or other place that they like to visit.

- Make a list of the places they name on a chart and hang the chart on the wall for children to see.

- Invite children to draw a picture of their favorite place. They may want to include a drawing of themselves and the sea horse in the picture.

- Have them use the list to write the name of the place on their illustration.

- Have children share their drawing with a friend.

Sugar Cookie Sea Horses

Art Standard: *Explores a variety of techniques to create original work*

- Slice a roll of refrigerated sugar cookie dough into one-half-inch slices. Provide each child with two slices.

- Have children make the body of a sea horse by rolling one slice of cookie dough into a ball and then flattening it into a circle on a piece of waxed paper.

- Have children make two smaller balls of dough from the second slice. Then have them flatten one ball of dough above the body for the head. Encourage them to shape the head like a horse's head. Then have them use a toothpick to make a hole in the dough for the eye.

- Have children roll the remaining dough ball into a snake. Then have them curl the dough so it looks like a sea horse tail. Press one end to the body.

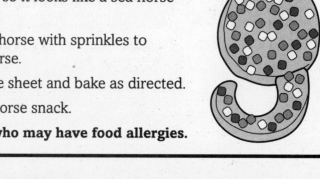

- Invite children to cover the sea horse with sprinkles to resemble the scales on a sea horse.

- Place the sea horses on a cookie sheet and bake as directed.

- Invite children to eat their sea horse snack.

Caution: Be aware of children who may have food allergies.

www.harcourtschoolsupply.com

22
Sea Horses: Writing Activity and Snack Idea
Sensational Seasons: Summer, SV 9781419033940

Math Center

Math Standard:
Demonstrates a beginning understanding of measurement using non-standard units and measurement words

Measuring Sea Horses

- Reduce and enlarge 6 sea horses (p. 26) that are each different lengths from three to ten inches long. Color each one a different color. Laminate and cut out the sea horses.

- Read an informational book about sea horses to children. Discuss with them that there are many different kinds of sea horses that vary in length from 1½ inches long to 14 inches long.

- Invite children to use inch cubes to find the length of each sea horse.

- Ask children to answer questions such as *What color was the longest sea horse?* or *How many cubes long was the yellow sea horse?*

Language Center

Language Arts Standard:
Recognizes rhyming words

Rhyming Sea Horses

- Duplicate six to eight sea horses (p. 25). Color and cut them out.

- Duplicate six to eight pairs of rhyming picture cards (pp. 6–8). Cut out and glue one picture card from each rhyming pair to a sea horse. Laminate the sea horses and remaining picture cards for durability.

- Challenge children to match the picture cards to the rhyming pictures on the sea horses.

Sea Horses: Centers
Sensational Seasons: Summer, SV 9781419033940

Art Center

Art Standard:
Explores a variety of
techniques to create
original work

Torn Paper Sea Horses

- Duplicate a sea horse (p. 25) on white construction paper for each child. Enlarge it if desired.

- Discuss with children how sea horses are an unusual kind of fish. They are covered with scales that are fused together to form an exoskeleton.

- Have children cut out the sea horse.

- Invite them to cover their sea horse with torn pieces of construction paper to resemble the rough texture of the scales.

- Have children glue a wiggly eye on their sea horse when they have finished covering the body with scales.

Science Center

Science Standard:
Displays curiosity
about animals

The Scales of a Sea Horse

- Duplicate the sea horse (p. 25) for use as a template. Trace the sea horse on a sturdy piece of cardboard. Squeeze a line of glue around the edge of the sea horse shape on the cardboard. Squeeze a large dot of glue on the sea horse shape for the eye. Then squeeze vertical and horizontal lines of glue over the entire body of the sea horse to resemble scales. Allow the glue to dry.

- Display books or pictures of sea horses that show the scales on a sea horse. Discuss with children how the scales form an outside skeleton, or exoskeleton.

- Provide children with crayons and thin newsprint paper.

- Invite children to place newsprint paper on top of the cardboard sea horse and secure it in place with a clothespin at each corner.

- Have them use a crayon to rub across the paper from top to bottom.

- Encourage children to look for the scales as the sea horse is revealed on the paper.

Sea Horse and Pouch Patterns

Use with "Daddy Sea Horse" on page 20, "Rhyming Sea Horses" on page 23,
"Torn Paper Sea Horses" on page 24, and "The Scales of a Sea Horse" on page 24.

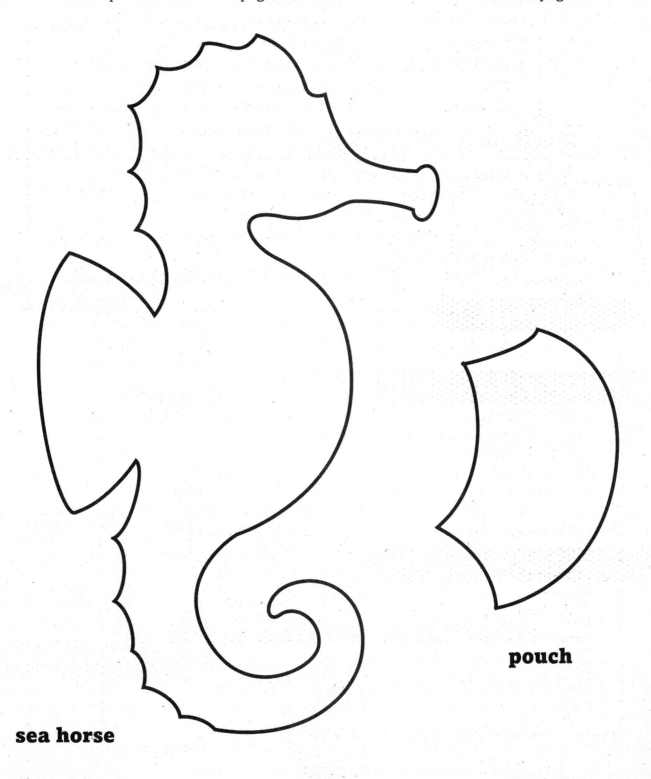

pouch

sea horse

Sea Horses: Patterns
Sensational Seasons: Summer, SV 9781419033940

Letter Cards

Use with "*Sea* Begins with *S*, and *Horse* Begins with *H*" on page 20.

Sea Horse Pictures

Use with "Measuring Sea Horses" on page 23.

sea horses

Sea Horses: Patterns
Sensational Seasons: Summer, SV 9781419033940

Camping Fun

Books to Read

A Camping Spree with Mr. Magee by Chris Van Dusen (Chronicle Books)

Bailey Goes Camping by Kevin Henkes (HarperTrophy)

Camping in the Temple of the Sun by Lesley Gould (Simon and Schuster Children's Publishing)

Curious George Goes Camping by H. A. Rey (Houghton Mifflin)

I Can Go Camping by Edana Eckart (Children's Press)

Just Me and My Dad by Mercer Mayer (Western Publishing)

Maisy Goes Camping by Lucy Cousins (Candlewick Press)

When Daddy Took Us Camping by Julie Brillhart (Albert Whitman & Company)

When We Go Camping by Margriet Ruurs (Tundra Books)

Camping Facts

In 2003 about 28 percent of the United States population went camping. However, it is estimated that only about 6 percent walked more than a quarter of a mile from their car to make a camp. Some of the national parks most often visited by campers include the Great Smoky Mountains, Grand Canyon, and Yosemite. Items that campers use include tents, sleeping bags, lanterns, insect repellent, and cooking gear and supplies. Campers also need fresh water to drink and cook with. Good campers are courteous to others by disposing of their trash in an environmentally friendly way and by leaving their campsite clean. It is important to use fire safety rules when building or cooking over a campfire.

Camping: Book List and Teacher Information
Sensational Seasons: Summer, SV 9781419033940

Sleeping Under the Stars

Materials

- black and brown craft paper
- border
- variety of colors of construction paper
- gold glitter
- old wallpaper samples
- brown, red, yellow, and orange tempera paint
- paintbrushes
- yarn
- hole punch
- scissors
- crayons or markers
- glue
- stapler

Directions

Teacher Preparation: Cover the top half of the bulletin board with black craft paper and the bottom half with brown craft paper. Provide each child with a six-inch by nine-inch construction paper, a six-inch by seven-inch piece of wallpaper, a three-inch circle, and a three-inch yellow star. Staple the wallpaper to the construction paper to resemble a sleeping bag. Paint a campfire on the brown section of the bulletin board using the picture on page 35 as a model. Add a border and the caption.

1. Have children spread a thin layer of glue on the star shape and cover it with glitter. Set the star aside to dry.

2. Have children punch holes about one inch apart around the edges of the wallpaper that is stapled to construction paper. Younger children may need help.

3. Tie one end of a long piece of yarn to the top corner of the sleeping bag.

4. Invite children to sew the yarn through the holes around the three edges of the sleeping bag, leaving the top open. Help them tie the yarn and trim if necessary.

5. Then have children use crayons or markers to draw a sleeping face on the circle. Glue the face on the sleeping bag.

6. Staple the stars on the black section of the bulletin board. Arrange the sleeping bags around the campfire on the brown section.

Going Camping

Language Arts Standard: *Shows awareness that different words begin with the same sound*

• Put the following toys or real items in a box: a backpack, binoculars, a fishing pole, a flashlight, a small cooler, a canteen, a sleeping bag, sunscreen, a trash bag, and a tent. Pictures of these items can be used if real or toy ones are not available.

• Read aloud an informational book about camping from the list on page 27.

• Invite children to take out one item from the box and say its name. Have them hold the item in their lap or place it in front of them.

• Have children take turns identifying the beginning sound of the name of the item that they are holding.

• Challenge them to find an item from the box that has the same beginning sound as their item. Have them sit next to the child who is holding that item.

• Make a list of word pairs on the board that begin with the same sound.

Marshmallows on a Stick

Math Standard: *Rote counts to 10*

• Provide children with a kabob skewer and a small handful of mini-marshmallows on a paper plate. Discuss safe ways to handle the skewer.

• For dramatic effect, make a campfire using sticks and red, yellow, and orange tissue paper. Have children sit in a circle around the "campfire."

• Name a number from 1 to 10 or hold up a flash card showing a number.

• Invite children to put that number of marshmallows on their "stick" and "toast" them over the fire.

• Then have children pull their marshmallows off the stick and eat them.

• Repeat the activity with other numbers until all of the marshmallows are eaten.

Caution: Be aware of children who may have food allergies.

Looking at Letters and Words

Language Arts Standard: *Demonstrates some ability to hear separate syllables in words*

• Write the word *campfire* on the board. Have children tell what words they hear in the word *campfire* (*camp* and *fire*).

• Invite children to say the word slowly and segment the syllables (*camp-fire*).

• Have children clap the syllables as they say the syllables. Then have children blend the word *campfire* back together.

• Encourage children to clap and count the syllables for other words, such as *binoculars, tent, backpack, lantern,* and *canoe.*

Sensational Seasons: Summer, SV 9781419033940

Stories Around the Campfire

Language Arts Standard: *Communicates ideas and thoughts*

- Discuss with children how campers enjoy sitting around the campfire and telling stories.
- Have children gather sticks on a pizza pan and make a campfire. Put pieces of red, yellow, and orange tissue paper between the sticks for the fire. Set the pizza pan with the fire on the floor and have children sit with you in a circle around the campfire.
- Begin telling a story such as *I got the tent out of the car and set it up. Then I went to get....*
- Invite the child sitting next to you to add a few lines to the story.
- Continue going around the circle until each child has had a turn to contribute to the story. Younger children may need guidance.
- Have a volunteer add the last few lines to conclude the story.

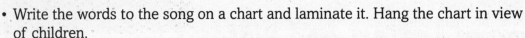

In Tune with Language

Language Arts Standard: *Begins to recognize high-frequency words*

- Invite children to learn the following song to the tune of "Hi, Ho, the Dairy-O."

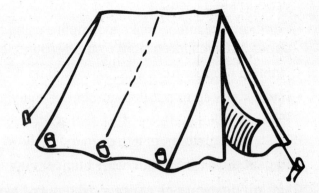

A-camping we will go.
A-camping we will go.
Grab your tent and sleeping bag!
A-camping we will go.

A-hiking we will go.
A-hiking we will go.
Grab your pack and binoculars!
A-hiking we will go.

A-canoeing we will go.
A-canoeing we will go.
Grab your boat and paddle, too!
A-canoeing we will go.

- Write the words to the song on a chart and laminate it. Hang the chart in view of children.
- Make word cards for the high-frequency words in the song such as *we, will,* and *go.* Hang the word cards next to the chart.
- Challenge children to find the high-frequency words in the song and circle them with a washable marker.
- Wipe off the chart with a damp paper towel or sponge and repeat the activity if desired.

When I Go Camping

Language Arts Standard: *Organizes writing from left to right*

- Invite children to name one item that they would need to go camping.

- Make a list of the items on chart paper by writing the following sentence for each response. *I will take a* _____ . Write children's names at the end of their sentence.

- Have children follow along as you read aloud all of the sentences.

- Cut the sentences apart and give children their sentence.

- Encourage them to write the words in their sentence on a sheet of drawing paper going from left to right.

- Then have children draw a picture of the item that they named.

Hiking Trail Mix

Science Standard: *Uses senses to observe and explore materials*

- Tell children that sometimes people who are camping enjoy going on a hike. They take water with them to drink when they get thirsty and a snack to eat that gives them energy.

- Place each of the following food items in a bowl with a spoon: multi-grain, oat cereal rings; pretzel sticks; nuts; raisins or other dried fruit; sunflower seeds; and small chocolate candies.

- Provide each child with a plastic bag.

- Invite children to put a spoonful of each food item into their bag to make trail mix.

- Have them make binoculars in the "Tube Binoculars" center on page 33, if desired.

- Have children take their binoculars, a bottle of water, and their trail mix and go on a hike around the school. Have them carry their items in a backpack made by putting their arms through the handles of a plastic grocery bag.

- Designate a time during the hike for children to sit and eat their snack.

- Have children tell which was their favorite item in the trail mix. Challenge them to describe its taste and texture.

Caution: Be aware of children who may have food allergies.

www.harcourtschoolsupply.com
 31
Camping: Writing Activity **and Snack Idea**
Sensational Seasons: Summer, SV 9781419033940

Math Center

Math Standard:
Recognizes basic geometric shapes

Fishing for Shapes

- Duplicate 10 fish (p. 34) on colored construction paper. Draw a geometric shape such as a circle, triangle, square, or rectangle on the back of each fish. Laminate and cut out the fish. Attach a paper clip to the mouth of each fish.

- Tie an 18-inch piece of yarn or string to the end of a 2-foot dowel rod to make a fishing pole. Tie a small magnet to the other end of the yarn or string.

- Have children spread the fish on the floor. Tell them that they are on a camping trip and are going fishing.

- Invite them to catch a fish by lowering the magnet so that it attracts the paper clip.

- Have them name the shape on the back of the fish they catch. Then have them place the fish in a basket or pail.

- When all of the fish have been caught, have children name the shapes on all of the fish in the basket or pail.

Language Center

Language Arts Standard:
Uses writing skills to convey meaning and information

Bird-Watching

- Duplicate eight birds (p. 34) on white construction paper. Color each bird one of the eight basic colors and write the name of the corresponding color word on the line below the birds. Laminate and cut them out.

- Tape the birds on the wall in various places around the room.

- Provide toy binoculars or have children make binoculars in the "Tube Binoculars" center on page 33. Also make available a clipboard with paper and a pencil.

- Tell children that campers sometimes enjoy bird-watching. It is fun to see how many different kinds of birds they can see.

- Invite children to use the binoculars to find the birds around the room.

- Challenge children to write the name of the color of each bird they see on the clipboard.

Art Center

Art Standard:
Writes recognizable letters in own name

Tube Binoculars

- Provide each child with two empty bathroom tissue tubes. Tape the two tubes together. Also provide each child with a two-foot piece of yarn.
- Cut colored construction paper into 4½ x 10 inch pieces.
- Invite children to write their name on the construction paper and then decorate it with stickers, markers, or crayons.
- Have children wrap the construction paper around the two tubes and glue it in place.
- Help them punch a hole, about one-half inch from the top, on each side of the tubes.
- Help children tie each end of the yarn through a hole.

Science Center

Science Standard:
Uses senses to observe and explore materials

Sensing in Nature

- Duplicate the activity master (p. 35). Provide a copy for each child.
- Discuss with children things that they might see or hear at night while camping.
- Invite them to color the pictures on the activity master.
- Then have children draw a circle around the sense they would use to learn more about each item on the activity master while camping at night.

Fish Pattern
Use with "Fishing for Shapes" on page 32.

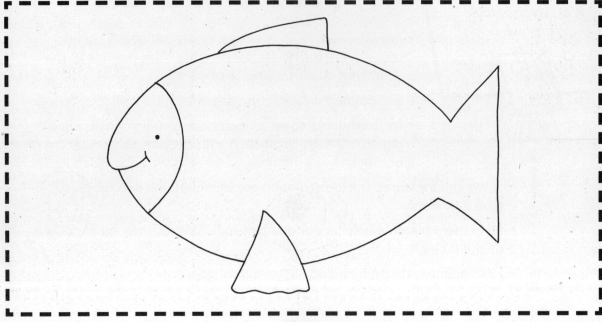

fish

Bird Pattern
Use with "Bird-Watching" on page 32.

bird

Name _____

Nighttime Senses

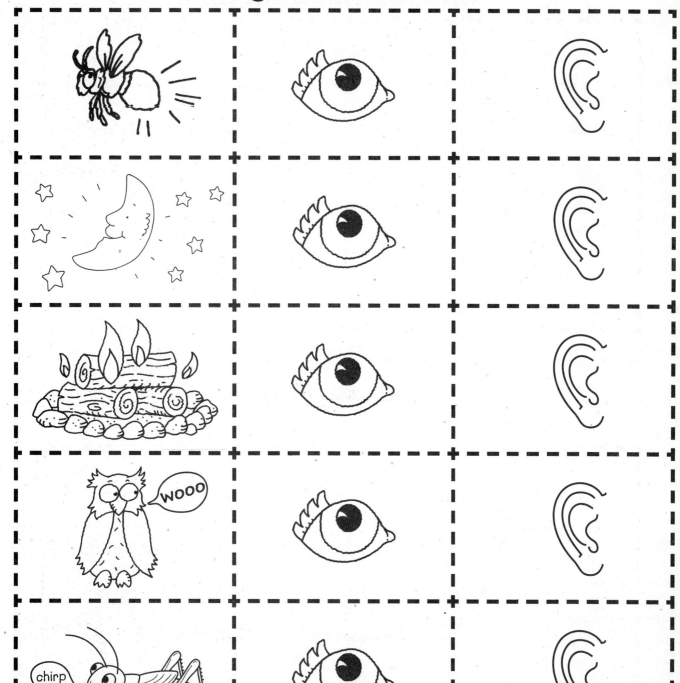

Directions: Use with "Sensing in Nature" on page 33. Have children color the pictures. Then have them circle the sense they would use to identify each item while camping at night.

Camping: Activity Master
Sensational Seasons: Summer, SV 9781419033940

Hi, Ho, the Dairy-O

Books to Read

- *Belinda* by Pamela Allen (Puffin)
- *Cock-a-Doodle-Moo!* by Bernard Most (Harcourt Children's Books)
- *Cow* by Jules Older (Charlesbridge Press)
- *Cows Can't Fly* by David Milgrim (Puffin)
- *From Cow to Ice Cream* by Bertram T. Knight (Children's Press)
- *Kiss the Cow!* by Phyllis Root (Candlewick)
- *Milk: From Cow to Carton* by Aliki (HarperTrophy)
- *The Milk Makers* by Gail Gibbons (Aladdin Books)
- *When Bluebell Sang* by Lisa Campbell Ernst (Aladdin)
- *When Cows Come Home* by David L. Harrison (Boys Mill Press)

Cow Facts

June is National Dairy Month and a good time to learn about milk and dairy products. Cows are mammals that are often called cattle. The adult male is a bull, and the female is called a cow. The female feeds her baby, called a calf, milk from her udder. Dairy cows are farm animals that are raised mostly for their milk from which other products like cheese and cream are made. Cattle may be white, black, brown, or tan. Some cattle have horns and others do not. They use their long tail to keep insects off their back. Cattle eat grass that they swallow without chewing. They later regurgitate a cud and chew more thoroughly before swallowing. Cattle are ruminants, which are animals that have a four-part stomach.

Sensational Seasons: Summer, SV 9781419033940

We're Just "Moo-ving" Along

Materials

- completed cows from "Milk Makers" on page 42
- light blue craft paper
- border
- white and green tempera paint
- paintbrushes
- sponge roller brushes
- scissors
- stapler
- newspapers

Directions

Teacher Preparation: Cut the blue craft paper to the size of the bulletin board. Draw a wavy line across the length of the blue paper that is about a third of the distance from the top edge. Cover a wall or floor area with newspapers to prepare a painting center.

1. Invite children to use a roller brush to paint the bottom two-thirds of the craft paper green to resemble a pasture. Allow paint to dry.

2. Have them use a paintbrush to paint a white fence across the green edge of the pasture.

3. Cover the bulletin board with the painted craft paper.

4. Staple the completed cows in a pleasing arrangement.

5. Staple a border and add the caption to the bulletin board.

Learning "Moo-re" About Cows

Language Arts Standard: *Relates prior knowledge to new information*

- Make a KWL chart showing three columns. Write the words KNOW, WANT to know, and LEARNED as headers for each column.

- Have children tell things they know about cows. Write their responses in the KNOW column.

- Ask children to tell things they want to know about cows. Guide children to ask questions such as *What does a cow eat?* Write their responses in the WANT column.

- Read children an informational book about cows from the book list on page 36.

- Invite children to complete the LEARNED column of the chart by telling things that they learned about cows after reading the book.

Our Favorite Dairy Foods

Math Standard: *Counts with understanding and recognizes "how many" in sets of objects*

- Invite children to taste several different dairy products such as cheese, yogurt, butter, and chocolate milk.

- Create a class graph from craft paper and label a column for each food item that children taste.

- Duplicate several copies of each child's class photo for use on the graph.

- Have children use double-sided tape to attach their photo under each heading of the dairy products that they like.

- Have volunteers count how many children liked each food.

- Ask the questions *Which food did children like the most? The least?*

Caution: Be aware of children who may have food allergies.

Looking at Letters and Words

Language Arts Standard: *Shows awareness that different words begin with the same sound*

- Name each letter as you write the word *milk* on the board.

- Have children find the letter *Mm* on the classroom alphabet picture cards. Talk about the key word picture that is used for *Mm*. Point out that the word begins with the same sound and letter as *milk*.

- Say the following word pairs. Invite children to say "moo" if both words begin with the /m/ sound. They should remain silent if the words begin with different sounds.

milk—money	**milk—mouse**	**milk—mother**
milk—garden	**milk—barn**	**milk—monster**

Milk Is "Moo-tritious"

Language Arts Standard: *Listens effectively in informal situations*

• Read aloud an informational book about cows. Tell children that we drink milk because it contains nutrients that we need for good health. Discuss with children that milk contains nutrients that help us grow, give us energy, and strengthen our bones and teeth.

• In a bag or box, place a real bone or a picture of a skeleton, some type of ball such as a soccer ball, and a tape measure.

• Place the bag or box in front of children. Tell them that there are clues inside that tell them why milk is good for them.

• Invite volunteers to take turns removing one item from the bag or box.

• Challenge children to guess the meaning of each clue. Guide them to the following conclusions.

the bone: milk strengthens our bones and teeth
the ball: milk gives us energy to work and play
the tape measure: milk helps us grow

In Tune with Language

Language Arts Standard: *Actively participates in songs*

• Read aloud an informational book from the book list (p. 36) such as *The Milk Makers* by Gail Gibbons.

• Invite children to sing the following song to the tune of "Here We Go 'Round the Mulberry Bush."

This is the way the cow eats grass, the cow eats grass, the cow eats grass.
This is the way the cow eats grass so early in the morning.

This is the way we milk the cow. . .
This is the way we drink the milk. . .

What the Little Calf Saw

Language Arts Standard: *Makes illustrations to match sentences*

- Lead a discussion with children about cattle. Tell them that the males are called bulls, the females are called cows, and the babies are called calves.

- Tell children the following story about a little calf.

  One morning, a little spotted calf woke up early just as the sun was coming up. It decided to walk through the pasture down to the pond to get a drink of water. On the way, the calf saw. . .

- Invite children to write or dictate a sentence telling what the calf saw on its way to the pond.

- Have them illustrate their sentence using crayons or markers.

- You may wish to staple the drawings together to make a class book for the reading center.

"Udder-ly" Delicious Butter

Science Standard: *Uses senses to observe and explore materials*

- Discuss with children foods that are made from milk. Tell them that butter is made from the fatty part of milk that is called cream.

- Fill a clean baby food jar with heavy cream and seal the lid tightly.

- Have children sit in a circle. Encourage them to take turns shaking the jar vigorously as they sing the song below to the tune of "Frère Jacques." Have them insert their name when it is their turn to shake the jar.

  _____ shakes it.
  _____ shakes it.
  Make some butter, make some butter.

  _____ shakes it.
  _____ shakes it.
  Make some butter, make some butter.

- Continue having children take turns shaking the jar until the cream separates into pale yellow clumps. Pour off the remaining liquid.

- Invite children to spread a dab of butter on a cracker for a tasty snack. You may wish to also have them try some store-bought butter and compare the taste.

Caution: Be aware of children who may have food allergies.

Sensational Seasons: Summer, SV 9781419033940

Math Center

Math Standard:
Uses concepts that include number recognition and counting

"Cow-culating" Numbers

- Duplicate ten cows and ten buckets (p. 43) on white construction paper.
- Write a number from 1 to 10 on each of the buckets.
- Then use a black ink pad to make a corresponding number of fingerprint spots on each cow.
- Invite children to match the buckets and cows that have the same numbers.

Language Center

Language Arts Standard:
Begins to understand alphabetical order

Lining Up the Cows

- Duplicate 26 cows (p. 43) on white construction paper. Color the cows with black spots to resemble dairy cows.
- Write a letter of the alphabet on each cow. Laminate the cows and cut them out.
- Write the letters of the alphabet in order on a sentence strip.
- Invite children to look at the sentence strip and use it to put the cows in a line in alphabetical order.

Sensational Seasons: Summer, SV 9781419033940

Art Center

Art Standard:
Creates representations
that contain
increasing detail

Milk Makers

- Duplicate a nose (p. 44) on pink construction paper for each child. Also duplicate two ears (p. 44) on white construction paper and two horns (p. 44) on brown construction paper for each child.

- Provide each child with a half sheet and two quarter sheets of white construction paper. Also give them a quarter sheet of pink construction paper.

- Have children glue a quarter sheet of white construction paper (the head) to the top corner of the half sheet (the body).

- Have children cut out the two ears and glue them to the sides of the head. Color the inside of the ears pink.

- Invite children to cut out the two horns and glue them to the top of the head.

- Have children cut out the nose and glue it on the lower part of the head. Then have them draw eyes and nostrils on the cow.

- Have children cut out four legs and a tail from a quarter sheet of white paper. The width of the legs will vary. Have children glue the legs and tail to the body.

- Encourage children to draw and cut out an udder on pink construction paper. Then have them glue the udder to the cow.

- Have children make large spots on their cow with black markers or paint.

Science Center

Science Standard:
Uses senses to observe
and explore materials

Milking Fun

- Read aloud an informational book that has pictures of cows being milked either by hand or by machine.

- Prepare three or four latex gloves for children to "milk." Blow air into each glove and poke the fingertips with a straight pin. Then fill each glove with a thin solution of white tempera paint and water. Secure the gloves by wrapping a rubber band tightly around the wrist opening.

- Invite children to hold a glove over a bucket and grasp one of the fingers near the top and gently pull downward to "milk" the cow.

Cow Pattern

Use with "'Cow-culating' Numbers" on page 41 and with "Lining Up the Cows" on page 41.

cow

Bucket Pattern

Use with "'Cow-culating' Numbers" on page 41.

bucket

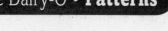

Nose, Ear, and Horn Patterns
Use with "Milk Makers" on page 42.

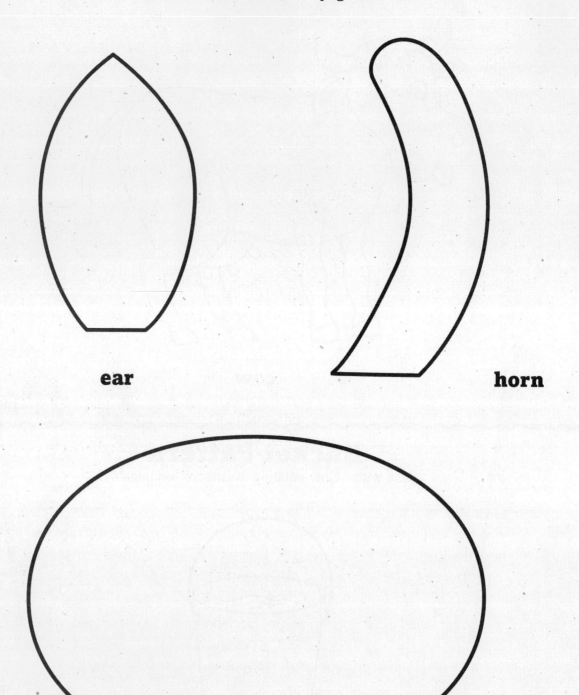

ear

horn

nose

Sensational Seasons: Summer, SV 9781419033940

Fireworks, Flags, and the Fourth

Books to Read

America the Beautiful by Lucy Cousins (Candlewick Press)

Apple Pie Fourth of July by Janet S. Wong (Harcourt Children's Books)

Happy 4th of July, Jenny Sweeney by Leslie Kimmelman (Albert Whitman & Co.)

Hats Off for the Fourth of July by Harriet Ziefert (Viking)

Hooray for the Fourth of July by Wendy Watson (Clarion Books)

I Pledge Allegiance by Bill Martin, Jr. (Candlewick Press)

Parade by Donald Crews (Mulberry)

The Story Of America's Birthday by Patricia A. Pingry (Candy Cane Press)

This Land Is Your Land by Woody Guthrie (Little, Brown, and Company)

Independence Day Facts

Independence Day is a holiday in the United States that celebrates the adoption of the Declaration of Independence by the Continental Congress on July 4, 1776. Independence Day is also known as the Fourth of July and the birthday of the United States of America. The first Independence Day was celebrated on July 8, 1776, with songs, the ringing of the Liberty Bell, a parade, and the firing of cannons. The first official flag was ordered in 1777 and had 7 red and 6 white alternating stripes. It had 13 stars on a field of blue to represent the 13 colonies that signed the Declaration of Independence. The Fourth of July is still celebrated today with parades, but fireworks have replaced the firing of cannons.

Sensational Seasons: Summer, SV 9781419033940

We Love the Red, White, and Blue

Materials

- white and red craft paper
- border
- red and blue tempera paint
- star pattern (p. 52)
- white construction paper
- copies of individual photos of children
- yardstick
- scissors
- glue
- stapler

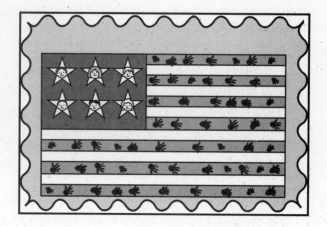

Directions

Teacher Preparation: Cover the bulletin board with red craft paper. Add a border and the caption. Cut a large, rectangular piece of white craft paper that covers all of the bulletin board except for the border and the caption. Lay the paper on a table and use a yardstick to draw lines that designate the field of blue and the stripes on the United States flag. Duplicate stars on white construction paper. Depending on the size of the bulletin board, there may not be space for 50 stars. Use the number of stars that looks pleasing. Duplicate children's class photos.

1. Paint each child's hand blue. Have children press a handprint with fingers together on the designated area. Guide them to place handprints close together and make as many rows as necessary to fill the blue area. Each child may need to make several handprints, depending on the number of children.

2. Have children wash their hands as needed.

3. Repeat the process using the red paint. Have them place their red handprints horizontally in rows to form the seven red stripes of the flag.

4. Invite children to cut out two or three stars each to total the amount needed.

5. Have them cut around their individual photo so that it will fit on a star. Have them glue their photo to a star.

6. Help children glue the stars in the blue area according to the United States flag. They may choose where to place the star with their picture.

7. Staple the completed flag on the bulletin board below the caption.

The United States of America

Language Arts Standard: *Identifies labels and signs in the environment*

- Show children an object that has a label that says *Made in the USA*.
- Have children tell if they have ever seen these letters and if they know what they stand for.
- Write *United States of America* on the board. Tell children that this is the name of our country. Sometimes the first letters of each word, or the initials, are used when writing our country's name.
- Challenge children to find other places at home or in the community where the letters *USA* are used.
- Make a list of the places where they found the letters used.

One Great Country

Language Arts Standard: *Communicates information with others*

- Tell children that the Fourth of July is a national holiday during which time people celebrate our country, the United States of America. Explain that the Fourth of July is like a big birthday party for our country.
- Show children pictures of some of the main symbols of the Fourth of July, such as the American flag, picnics, fireworks, and parades.
- Read aloud a book such as *Parade* by Donald Crews.
- Invite children to tell about a time they watched a parade or a fireworks show.

Looking at Letters and Words

Language Arts Standard: *Demonstrates some ability to hear separate syllables in words*

- Read children a book such as *I Pledge Allegiance* by Bill Martin, Jr., that explains the meanings of the words used in the pledge.
- Write a word from the pledge such as *republic* on the board. Invite children to say the word slowly and segment the syllables (*re-pub-lic*).
- Have children clap the syllables as they say them and then blend the word *republic* back together.
- Challenge children to clap and count the syllables for other words, such as *pledge, allegiance, flag, nation,* and *liberty*.
- Demonstrate for children how to place their hand on their heart when they say the pledge, symbolizing that they are telling the truth.
- Invite them to stand and face the classroom flag and say the pledge each day.

Hooray for the Red, White, and Blue

Math Standard: *Counts objects using one-to-one correspondence*

- Use an overhead projector to draw a large flag that is about 2 feet by 3 feet on white craft paper. Color the upper left-hand corner blue. Make 50 dots on the blue field that copy the layout of the stars on the United States flag. Cut out 50 white stars that are in proportion to the size of the flag. Also cut 7 red stripes that match the size of the flag.

- Invite children to name the country that they live in, eliciting the United States of America. Tell children that all countries have a flag that is the symbol of the country.

- Hang the classroom flag in easy view of children. Lay the large white flag on the floor and have children sit around it.

- Invite children to place the red paper stripes on the flag using the classroom flag as a guide. Glue the stripes in place.

- Have children glue a star on each of the 50 dots in the blue field.

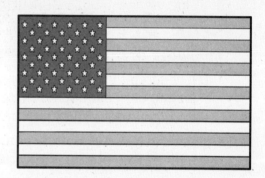

- Have children count how many red and how many white stripes are on the flag.

- Have them count how many stars are in each row. Challenge them to find out how many rows have 6 stars and how many rows have 5 stars. Encourage children to count all 50 stars.

- Hang the flag on the wall next to the classroom flag.

In Tune with Language

Language Arts Standard: *Understands that reading progresses from left to right*

- Write the words to the song "My Country 'Tis of Thee" on chart paper.

  My country 'tis of thee,
  Sweet land of liberty,
  Of thee I sing.
  Land where my fathers died,
  Land of the Pilgrim's pride,
  From every mountainside
  Let freedom ring.

- Read the words to children, pointing to the words as you read them from left to right.

- Tell children this is a patriotic song about America. Talk about the meaning of the song. Explain that many people died in the Revolutionary War so that America could be a free country.

- Remind children about the Pilgrims, who came to this country seeking religious freedom.

- Talk about the word *freedom* with children.

Names on Parade

Language Arts Standard: *Uses scribbles, approximations of letters, or known letters to represent written language*

• Duplicate enough parade floats (p. 52) to equal the number of letters in each child's name.

• Invite children to write the letters of their name on the parade floats, making sure that there is one letter on each float.

• Have children color the floats and cut them out.

• Have children glue the floats on a sentence strip in the correct sequence.

• If desired, measure the sentence strip and staple the ends together to make a headband for children to wear.

Patriotic Yogurt Cups

Math Standard: *Counts objects using one-to-one correspondence*

• Discuss with children how the colors red, white, and blue are symbolic colors that are on the U.S. flag.

• Provide each child with a plastic cup filled halfway with vanilla yogurt and a spoon.

• Put blueberries, sliced strawberries, and banana slices in separate bowls.

• Invite children to count out five blueberries and put them on their yogurt.

• Have children put three banana slices and three strawberry slices on their yogurt.

• Then have children stir the fruit into the yogurt.

• Encourage children to enjoy their patriotic snack.

Caution: Be aware of children who may have food allergies.

Math Center

Math Standard:
Translates a pattern from one representation to another

Red, White, and Blue Bracelets

- Cut several red, white, and blue one-inch squares. Glue the squares on index cards to represent a few familiar patterns that include the three colors (for example, red, white, blue, red, white, blue or red, red, blue, blue, white, white). Laminate the cards.

- Provide each child with an eight-inch piece of elastic cord that has a knot tied on one end.

- Put a generous supply of red, white, and blue pony beads in bowls.

- Invite children to choose a pattern card.

- Have them string beads on the elastic cord following the pattern indicated on their card.

- Tie the ends of the elastic cord together so that children can wear their red, white, and blue bracelet.

Language Center

Language Arts Standard:
Begins to recognize beginning sounds

Here Comes the Band!

- Duplicate the musical instruments and letters (p. 53). Cut them out and mount them on construction paper strips. Then laminate them.

- Have children name each musical instrument and identify the beginning sound in its name.

- Invite them to use a washable marker to circle the letters on each card that make the beginning sound in the name of each instrument.

- Have children use a damp sponge to wipe off the cards.

Art Center

Social Studies Standard:
Begins to identify customs associated with national patriotic holidays

July Fourth Headband

- Lead a discussion with children about Independence Day parades.
- Duplicate three stars (p. 52) on white construction paper for each child.
- Mark the center of a sentence strip with an X to indicate where to glue the center star. Cut several 18-inch red, white, and blue crepe paper streamers for each child.
- Have children cut out 3 stars and cover them with silver glitter.
- Have them glue the stars on the sentence strip with the middle star on the X.
- Have an adult measure the sentence strip and staple the ends together to make a headband.
- Have children glue the ends of several crepe paper strips to the back of the headband so that they hang freely.
- Invite children to wear their headband and parade around the school.

Sensory Center

Science Standard:
Uses senses to observe and explore materials

Patriotic Rice

- Divide a generous supply of rice into 3 plastic bags.
- Add 10 to 15 drops of red food coloring to one bag of rice and shake until the rice is tinted red. Allow the rice to dry.
- Repeat the same process with blue food coloring in a second bag.
- Pour all 3 bags of dry rice into a plastic tub and mix them together.
- Provide measuring spoons, cups, and funnels.
- Invite children to use the utensils to measure and pour the "patriotic" rice into the sensory tub.

Star Pattern

Use with "We Love the Red, White, and Blue" on page 46, "July Fourth Headband"
on page 51, and "Count Down to Blastoff" on page 57.

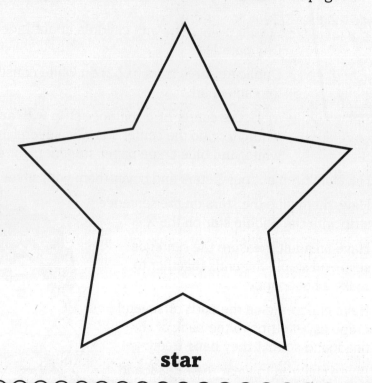

star

Float Pattern

Use with "Names on Parade" on page 49.

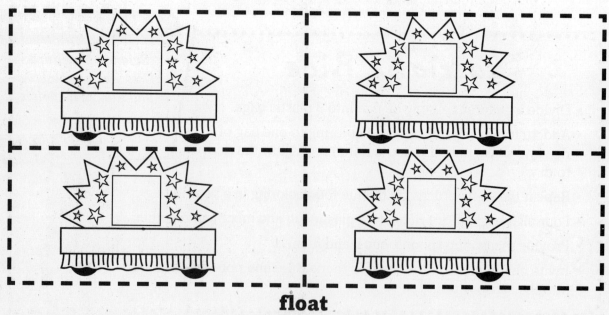

float

Musical Instruments and Letter Cards
Use with "Here Comes the Band!" on page 50.

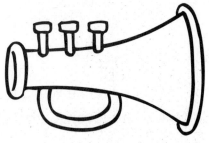

horn

h h h n

triangle

t f t t

drum

d b d d

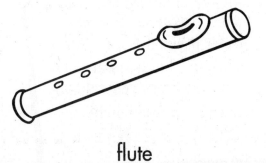

flute

f f f h

Independence Day: Patterns
Sensational Seasons: Summer, SV 9781419033940

Astronauts in Space

Books to Read

Big Silver Space Shuttle by Ken Wilson-Max (Cartwheel Books)

Floating in Space by Franklyn M. Branley (HarperCollins Juvenile Books)

I Want to Be an Astronaut by Byron Barton (HarperCollins Juvenile Books)

Looking into Space by Nigel Nelson (Reader's Digest)

Moon Man by Tomi Ungerer (Roberts Rinehart Publishers)

Papa, Please Get the Moon for Me by Eric Carle (Little Simon)

Roaring Rockets by Tony Mitton and Ant Parker (Turtleback Books)

The Moon Book by Gail Gibbons (Holiday House)

There's No Place Like Space: All About Our Solar System by Tish Rabe (Random House Books for Young Readers)

Zoom! Zoom! Zoom! I'm Off to the Moon by Dan Yaccarino (Scholastic)

Astronaut Facts

Prior to any humans going into space, the National Aeronautics and Space Administration sent a chimpanzee named Ham into space in 1961. A few months later, Alan B. Shepard, Jr., was the first American to leave Earth's atmosphere for a short period of 15 minutes. His tiny *Mercury* spacecraft splashed into the Atlantic for a safe return. The following year, John Glenn orbited Earth three times. Throughout the history of space travel, astronauts have continued to go into space. On July 29, 1969, the first astronauts walked on the moon. In 1981, the *Columbia* space shuttle was the first reused manned spacecraft. In 1998, the United States joined four other countries in constructing and manning the International Space Station. A crew of two or three, which rotates every few months, remains on the space station at all times.

Sensational Seasons: Summer, SV 9781419033940

Blasting Off into Space!

Materials

- rocket pattern (p. 61)
- pictures of various spacecraft, including rockets and the space shuttle
- black craft paper
- border
- red, yellow, and orange crepe paper streamers
- white construction paper
- crayons or markers
- gold or silver glitter
- scissors
- glue

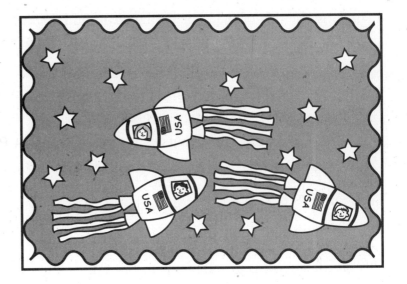

Directions

Teacher Preparation: Duplicate a rocket for each child on white construction paper. Cut black craft paper to fit the size of the bulletin board. Cut crepe paper streamers into narrow strips about six inches long.

1. Lead a discussion with children about how astronauts travel in space. Show children pictures of various spacecraft.

2. Invite children to put dots of glue on the black craft paper and sprinkle gold or silver glitter on the dots to resemble twinkling stars in space. Allow glue to dry and then cover the bulletin board with the paper. Add a border and the caption.

3. Have children decorate their rocket by drawing a face of an astronaut in the window. They may also write *USA* and draw a flag on the rocket.

4. Have them cut out their rocket.

5. Have children glue several streamers on the back of their rocket so that it looks like fire coming out of the engine.

6. Staple the rockets in a pleasing arrangement on the bulletin board.

I Want to Be an Astronaut

Language Arts Standard: *Begins to show awareness about concepts of print and word*

- Read aloud *I Want to Be an Astronaut* by Byron Barton. Other books about astronauts or space may be used if there is limited print and large print on the pages.
- Point out the title of the book on the cover and the title page to children.
- Have them point to where to begin reading on a page.
- Have them point to a period and tell why it is there.
- Write some familiar sight words from the book on word cards.
- Challenge children to find those words in the book.

Orbiting the Moon

Language Arts Standard: *Begins to understand and name opposites*

- Duplicate the rocket (p. 61), the earth (p. 62), and the moon (p. 62). Color, cut out, and laminate them.
- Duplicate an arrow (p. 62) for each child. Write a word that has an opposite on each arrow. Have children color and cut out their arrow.
- Use double-sided tape to place the earth and the moon on the wall several feet apart.
- Tape the rocket on the edge of the earth as though it is on a launch pad headed toward the moon.
- Tape the arrows in a path from the earth orbiting around the moon.
- Tell children that they are going to help the rocket go to the moon and return to the earth.
- Invite children to move the rocket to the first arrow.
- Read the word that is written on the arrow to children. Have them say the opposite of that word.
- Have children continue taking turns moving the rocket to the next arrow and saying the opposite until the rocket returns to the earth.

Sensational Seasons: Summer, SV 9781419033940

Count Down to Blastoff

Math Standard: *Counts backward from 10 to 1*

- Duplicate 11 stars (p. 52) on yellow construction paper. Write a number from 0 to 10 on each star. Laminate and cut the stars out. Attach magnetic tape to the back of each star.
- Discuss with children how mission control counts backward from 10 to 0 before liftoff.
- Have children arrange the stars in numerical order backward from 10 to 0 on a magnetic board.
- Invite children to stand and count backward from 10 to 0.
- Have them squat a little closer to the floor as they count each number.
- Have children jump up and say in a loud voice, "Blastoff!" when they get to 0.

Looking at Letters and Words

Language Arts Standard: *Begins to identify onsets and rimes*

- Have children blend together onsets and rimes to form words.
- Challenge them to say the word *moon* when you say *m–oon*.
- Repeat the activity with other space words like those listed below.

s–un	sp–ace	st–ar
l–aunch	z–oom	

In Tune with Language

Language Arts Standard: *Recognizes rhyming words*

- Invite children to learn the following song to the tune of "Eensy Weensy Spider."

**See the big space shuttle
On the launch pad.
The astronauts are ready,
And they are very glad
To put on their spacesuits
And climb aboard the ship.
Let's say the countdown
No number will we skip.
10, 9, 8, 7, 6, 5, 4, 3, 2, 1, 0 BLASTOFF!**

- Write the words *pad, glad, ship,* and *skip* on the board. Challenge children to name other words that rhyme with those listed and write them on the board.
- Have children name the common letters in the rhyming words.

Let's Write

Language Arts Standard: *Uses scribbles, approximations of letters, or known letters to represent written language*

- Read aloud *Zoom! Zoom! Zoom! I'm Off to the Moon* by Dan Yaccarino, which is about a little boy becoming an astronaut and taking a fantasy journey through space.

- Discuss with children how astronauts write in a journal or a logbook about the events that happen and the things they see while in space.

- Invite children to write or dictate a sentence about what they might see or do if they were an astronaut in space. The use of scribble writing by younger children is encouraged.

- Have them illustrate their sentence.

- Staple all of the pages together to make a class book and add a cover with the title *Our Space Log*.

- Place the book in the reading center for children.

Squishy Space Pudding

Science Standard: *Uses senses to observe and explore materials*

- Discuss with children how astronauts experience zero gravity while in space. Astronauts have to eat some foods in an unusual way because even their food floats.

- Have children measure one tablespoon of dry pudding mix and three tablespoons of milk into a quart-size resealable plastic bag.

- Have children squeeze the bag with their hands for about two minutes until ingredients are thoroughly mixed and the mixture is smooth.

- Help children cut off a very small piece of one corner of the bag.

- Invite them to squeeze pudding into their mouth like an astronaut.

Caution: Be aware of children who may have food allergies.

Sensational Seasons: Summer, SV 9781419033940

Math Center

Math Standard:
Counts objects using one-to-one correspondence

Collecting Moon Rocks

- Make available 20 to 30 rocks (about 1 inch to 2 inches in size), a pair of tongs, a number cube, and a large butter tub or bowl.

- Tell children that astronauts use a tong-like tool to pick up moon rocks. Their spacesuits are very bulky, which makes it impossible to bend down to pick up moon rocks.

- Have children spread the rocks on the table as though it is the surface of the moon.

- Invite them to take turns rolling the number cube to determine how many rocks they can collect.

- Have children use tongs to pick up rocks and place them in the butter tub or bowl.

- Encourage children to continue rolling the number cube until all of the rocks are collected.

Language Center

Language Arts Standard:
Begins to recognize letters of the alphabet

Rocket Letter Cards

- Duplicate a picture card for each letter of the alphabet. Write one uppercase or lowercase letter on each card. Glue the cards to construction paper, laminate them, and cut them out.

- Invite children to play with a partner. Have one partner stack the letter cards faceup, displaying the card on top of the deck.

- Have the other partner name the letter on the card.

- Have children keep the letter card in their own stack if they can name the letter correctly.

- Have children return the card to the bottom of the stack if they cannot name the letter correctly.

- Encourage children to continue playing as they take turns naming the letters.

Art Center

Art Standard:
Writes to communicate
for a variety of
purposes

Paper Bag Spacesuit

- Provide each child with a brown grocery bag and an empty cereal box. Cover the cereal box with white craft paper.

- Open the bag and help children cut the sides from the bag halfway up to allow room for their shoulders.

- Help them cut out a square hole for the face of the helmet on one side of the bag.

- Invite children to use markers to draw dials and patches on the bag.

- Have them label their spacesuit with *NASA* and *USA*. Explain the meanings.

- Have children glue the cereal box to the back of the bag to represent an air pack.

Science Center

Science Standard:
Begins to understand
about scientific
inquiry

Straw Rockets

- Provide each child with a small index card cut in half, a small drinking straw, a large drinking straw, and a pea-size ball of modeling clay.

- Invite children to draw a picture of a rocket on the index card and cut it out.

- Help them tape the rocket to one end of the large straw.

- Have them plug the same end of the straw with a pea-size ball of modeling clay.

- Then have children insert a small drinking straw halfway into the open end of the large straw.

- Invite them to blow through the small straw to launch the rocket.

Sensational Seasons: Summer, SV 9781419033940

Rocket Pattern
Use with "Blasting Off into Space!" on page 55 and "Orbiting the Moon" on page 56.

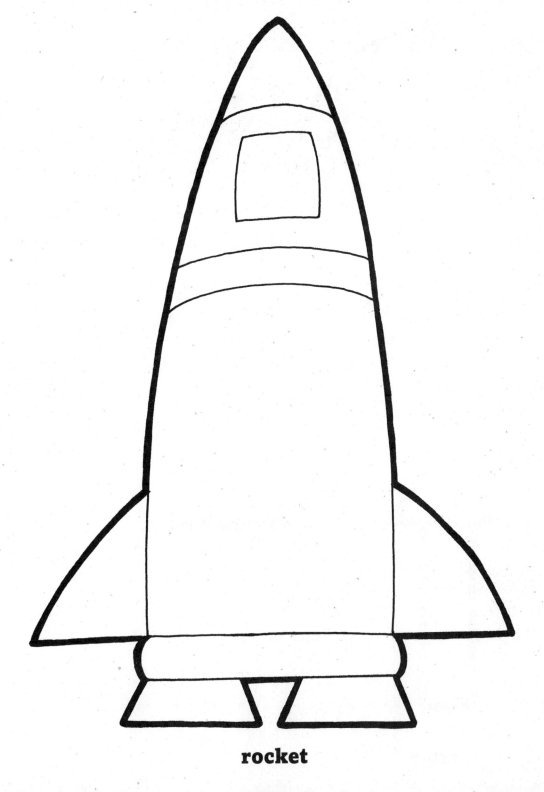

rocket

Astronauts: Patterns
Sensational Seasons: Summer, SV 9781419033940

Earth, Moon, and Arrow Patterns
Use with "Orbiting the Moon" on page 56.

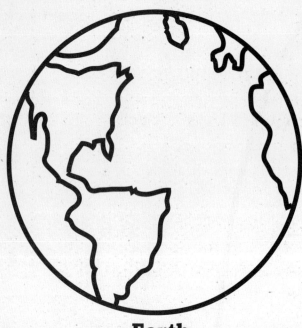

Earth

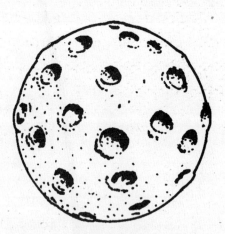

moon

arrow

Sensational Seasons: Summer, SV 9781419033940

Crazy Crocs and Alligators, Too

Books to Read

A Girl and Her Gator by Sean Bryan (Arcade Publishing)
Alligators All Around by Maurice Sendak (HarperTrophy)
Alligators & Crocodiles by John Bonnett Wexo (Wildlife Educator)
Baby Alligator by Ginjer L. Clarke (Grosset & Dunlap)
Counting Crocodiles by Judy Sierra (Rebound by Sagebrush)
Crocodile Beat by Gail Jorgensen (Aladdin)
Lyle, Lyle, Crocodile by Bernard Waber (Houghton Mifflin)
The Extraordinary Egg by Leo Lionni (Checkmark Books)
There's an Alligator Under My Bed by Mercer Mayer (Dial Books)

Crocodile and Alligator Facts

Alligators and crocodiles are reptiles, which are animals that are coldblooded, have scales, breathe air, and usually lay eggs. Alligators tend to have wide, rounded snouts, while crocodiles have longer, thin snouts. The fourth tooth on the lower jaw sticks up over the upper lip of the crocodile when its mouth is closed. This is not true of the alligator. Crocodiles and alligators use their powerful senses of smell, sight, and hearing to hunt their prey. They cannot chew, so they have to tear off large pieces of meat. They juggle the meat around until it falls down their throat. The fierce-looking reptilian moms take good care of their hatchlings. The female digs a nest, lays her eggs, carefully covers the eggs, and guards them until they hatch. After the young have hatched, the mom carries them to the water in her mouth and stays nearby to protect them for several months.

Sensational Seasons: Summer, SV 9781419033940

Down the River We Go

Materials

- alligator pattern (p. 71)
- blue craft paper
- border
- white and green construction paper
- green tempera paint
- paintbrushes
- large wiggly eyes
- glue
- stapler
- scissors
- black marker

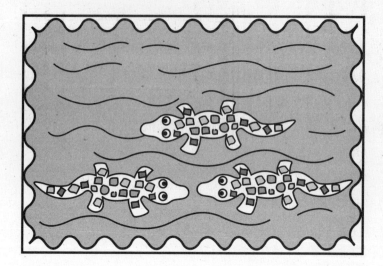

Directions

Teacher Preparation: Enlarge the alligator to the size of 9-inch by 12-inch construction paper. Duplicate an alligator on white paper for each child. Cover the bulletin board with blue craft paper. Use a black marker to draw wave lines indicating water. Add a border and the caption.

1. Cut out the alligator. Younger children may need help with cutting.

2. Completely cover the alligator with green paint.

3. Glue 2 wiggly eyes on the alligator's head.

4. Tear green construction paper into small pieces that are about 1-inch square.

5. Glue the torn paper pieces on the alligator to resemble scales.

6. Staple the alligators in a pleasing arrangement on the bulletin board.

Learning About Alligators and Crocodiles

Language Arts Standard: *Relates prior knowledge to new information*

- Make a KWL chart showing three columns. Write the words KNOW, WANT to know, and LEARNED as headers for each column.

- Have children tell things they know about alligators and crocodiles. Write their responses in the KNOW column.

- Have children tell things they want to know about alligators and crocodiles. Write their responses in the WANT column. Guide children to ask questions such as *How do they take care of their babies?*

- Read children an informational book about alligators and crocodiles from the book list on page 63.

- Invite them to complete the LEARNED column of the chart by telling things that they learned about alligators and crocodiles after reading the book.

Counting Eggs in the Nest

Math Standard: *Begins to compare groups and recognize more than, less than, and equal to relationships*

- Discuss with children how mother alligators and crocodiles make a nest for their eggs in the sand.

- Fill 2 shallow boxes halfway with sand to make 2 nests. Gather 12 table tennis balls and 2 large number cubes.

- Put 1 nest, 6 balls, and 1 of the number cubes on the floor in front of you. Have children sit in a circle so they can see the objects.

- Put the other nest, 6 balls, and 1 number cube in front of a child.

- Start by rolling the number cube. Put that number of "eggs" into your nest.

- Have the child who has the other nest follow the same procedure.

- Periodically, challenge the child to tell which nest has more eggs. Children will notice that sometimes both nests will have the same number of eggs.

- Have children pass the second nest around the circle and repeat the activity until everyone has had a turn.

- Encourage listening skills by randomly having children tell which nest has the least number of eggs.

Heads Up

Language Arts Standard: *Understands that letters make sounds*

- Duplicate the picture cards (pp. 6, 7, and 8). Cut them out and glue them on index cards in pairs. Make several cards that have pictures with the same beginning sounds, such as *bat* and *bell*. Also make several cards that have pictures with different beginning sounds, such as *pie* and *rug*. Put double-sided or magnetic tape on the back of each card.

- Show children pictures of alligators and crocodiles. Lead a discussion about how alligators' heads are wide and rounded while crocodiles' heads are long and thin.

- Duplicate the picture cards (p. 71) and laminate them. Stick double-sided or magnetic tape on the back of the cards and tape them to the board.

- Turn the remaining picture cards facedown and mix them up.

- Invite children to pick a card. Have them name the two pictures on their card.

- Have them put their card below the picture of the two heads that are the same if their pictures start with the same beginning sound.

- Have them put their card below the picture of the two heads that are different if their pictures have different beginning sounds.

In Tune with Language

Language Arts Standard: *Shows awareness that different words begin with the same sound*

- Invite children to act out the song below to the tune of "Five Little Monkeys Jumping on the Bed."

Five little monkeys swinging in a tree,
Teasing Mr. Alligator, "You can't catch me."
Along came Mr. Alligator quiet as can be
And scared that monkey right out of the tree!

(Repeat with 4 little monkeys, then 3, 2, 1, and 0.)

- Have children identify the beginning sounds for the words *monkey* and *alligator*.

- Write the words *monkey* and *alligator* on the board.

- Challenge children to name other words that begin with /a/ and /m/.

- Make a list of /a/ and /m/ words on the board.

Alliterative Alligators

Language Arts Standard: *Shows awareness that different words begin with the same sound*

- Show children pictures of alligators and crocodiles.

- Write the words *alligator* and *crocodile* on the board.

- Have children identify the beginning sound for each word.

- Invite them to draw a picture of an alligator or crocodile.

- Have children write or dictate an alliterative name for their drawing, such as *Alex Alligator* or *Carlos Crocodile*.

Alligator Applesauce

Math Standard: *Fills a shape with solids or liquids*

- Fill a bowl with enough applesauce for each child to have a one-half-cup serving.

- Have children watch as you mix several drops of green food coloring into the applesauce.

- Provide small bowls for the children. Invite them to spoon one-half cup of applesauce into a measuring cup and pour it into their bowl.

- Have children sprinkle a small amount of cinnamon on top of the applesauce.

- Have them stir it into the green applesauce to give it a texture like alligator skin.

- Invite children to eat their alligator applesauce.

Caution: Be aware of children who may have food allergies.

Math Center

Math Standard:
Demonstrates a beginning understanding of measurement using non-standard units and measurement words

The Long and Short of It

• Reduce and enlarge the alligator (p. 71) to five different lengths of four, five, six, seven, and eight inches. Color them and cut them out. Laminate for durability.

• Discuss with children how alligators and crocodiles are very small when they hatch. As they grow, some are longer than others.

• Provide children with inch cubes or paper clips.

• Invite children to measure each alligator to determine how many inch cubes or paper clips long they are.

• Challenge children to put the alligators in order from shortest to longest.

Language Center

Language Arts Standard:
Begins to recognize letters of the alphabet

Alligator Alphabet

• Duplicate an activity master (p. 70) for each child.

• Write the letters of the alphabet on a sentence strip.

• Challenge children to draw lines to connect the dots in alphabetical order to complete the picture. Have children use the alphabet on the sentence strip as a guide.

• Invite them to color the picture.

Art Center

Art Standard:
Explores a variety of techniques to create original work

Alligator Finger Puppet

- Duplicate the alligator and finger band (p. 71) on green construction paper for each child.

- Have children cut out the alligator and finger band. Younger children may need help with cutting.

- Invite children to spread a thin layer of glue on the alligator and sprinkle green glitter on it.

- Have children glue two wiggly eyes on the head.

- Staple the alligator to the middle of the finger band.

- Have children glue the ends of the finger band to fit their index finger.

Help the Hatchlings

Sensory Center

Science Standard:
Uses senses to observe and explore materials

- Set a tub of water near the sand table. Bury ten table tennis balls in sand. Provide a pair of kitchen tongs.

- Lead a discussion with children about how mother alligators and crocodiles protect their babies when they hatch by carrying them in their mouth to the water. The babies are safer from predators in the water.

- Have children pretend that the kitchen tongs are the mother's mouth. Invite children to dig up the balls or "hatchlings" with the kitchen tongs.

- Encourage children to pick up one hatchling at a time with the tongs and carry it to the water.

Alphabet Dot-to-Dot

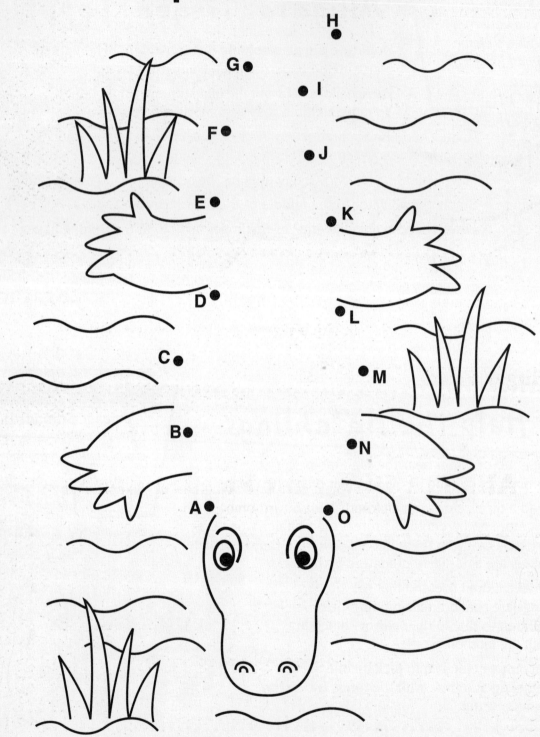

Directions: Use with "Alligator Alphabet" on page 68. Have children connect the dots to complete the alligator. Invite them to color the picture.

Alligator Patterns
Use with "Down the River We Go" on page 64, "The Long and Short of It"
on page 68, and "Alligator Finger Puppet" on page 69.

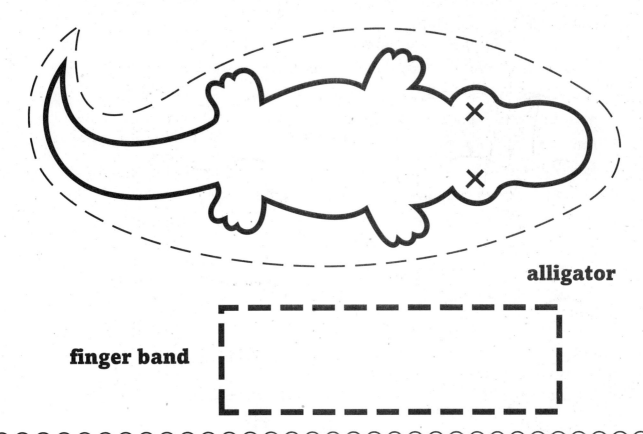

alligator

finger band

Alike or Different Picture Cards
Use with "Heads Up" on page 66.

same

different

71

Books to Read

A Day at the Beach: A Seaside Counting Book from One to Ten by Sandy Seeley Walling (Abernathy House Publishing)

Anno's Counting Book by Mitsumasa Anno (HarperCollins Juvenile Books)

How Many, How Many, How Many by Rick Walton (Candlewick Press)

How Many Snails?: A Counting Book by Paul Giganti (HarperTrophy)

Mouse Count by Ellen Stoll Walsh (Red Wagon Books)

My First Counting Book by Lilian Moore (Golden Books)

Ten Black Dots by Donald Crews (HarperTrophy)

The Cheerios Counting Book by Barbara McGrath (Cartwheel)

The Icky Bug Counting Book by Jerry Pallotta (Charlesbridge Publishing)

Number Facts

All cultures around the world have a system for counting. The very first numbers were actually pictures. Roman numerals were letters that stood for numbers. For example, the capital *I* stood for the number *one*. Two *I*s next to each other stood for the number *two*. Numbers were invented so that people would have a way to know what was bought and sold. Before numbers, people kept track of groups with stones. We use the numbers 0, 1, 2, 3, 4, 5, 6, 7, 8, and 9. Any larger number can be made using a combination of these numbers. The largest number is not known since numbers can go on indefinitely.

Numbers on Parade

Materials

- number patterns (p. 79 and p. 80)
- any color of craft paper
- border
- construction paper
- tempera paint
- paintbrushes
- scissors
- stapler

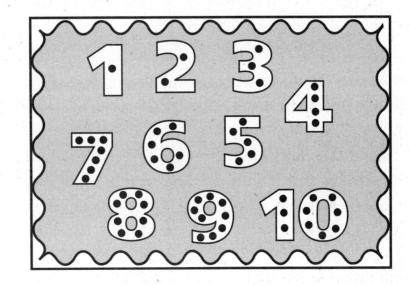

Directions

Teacher Preparation:

Enlarge the numbers to construction-paper size and duplicate. Provide each child with a number. Repeat the numbers if necessary. Cover the bulletin board with craft paper. Add a border and the caption. Set up a paint center.

1. Have children cut out a number.

2. Invite them to paint a corresponding number of large dots on their number cutout.

3. Staple the numbers in numerical order on the bulletin board in a zigzag row to resemble a parade. Repeat the numbers if necessary.

Numbers All Around

Language Arts Standard: *Seeks answers to questions*

- Show children a toy telephone, a small analog clock, and a calculator. Have children tell how these objects are alike. Guide them to say that they all have numbers on them.

- Lead a discussion with children about how numbers are used and how they allow us to count in many ways.

- Invite children to find ways that numbers are used in the classroom, such as counting the days on the calendar or counting the number of children in a center.

- Write the question *How many ways do we use numbers?* on a chart. Make a list of children's responses. Count how many responses are on the list.

Skip Counting

Language Arts Standard: *Listens with understanding and responds to directions*

- Duplicate the numbers (p. 79 and p. 80) on construction paper and cut them out.

- Prepare five blank cards by cutting three pieces of construction paper in half, leaving one extra.

- Introduce children to skip counting. Put the ten number cutouts in a row on the floor or on a table in front of children.

- Have children point to the numbers as they take turns counting to ten.

- Cover the number one with a blank card. Invite a child to skip the number two and cover up the three. Continue this procedure until all of the odd numbers are covered up.

- Explain that children covered a number, then skipped a number, and so on.

- Invite them to skip the numbers that are covered and count the ones that are showing.

Looking at Letters and Words

Language Arts Standard: *Begins to recognize high-frequency words*

- Write the number words *one* through *ten* on word cards.

- Invite ten children to hold up the word cards that correspond to the words in the nursery rhyme below.

  One, two, buckle my shoe.
  Three, four, shut the door.
  Five, six, pick up sticks.
  Seven, eight, lay them straight.
  Nine, ten, a big fat hen.

- Challenge children to say the rhyme again. This time tell them to mouth the number words and say the movements out loud.

A-Counting We Will Go

Math Standard: *Rote counts to 10*

- Have children stand in a circle.

- Select a number from 3 to 10 that will be the number to which the children will count.

- Explain to children that they are going to take turns counting aloud to the target number. Stand in the middle of the circle and point from child to child, going around the circle. As you point to each child, he or she will say the next number.

- Have the child that says the target number sit down where he or she is standing.

- Start counting again with the next child and continue until the target number is reached again. Have that child sit down.

- Continue counting to the target number around the circle until one child is left standing.

In Tune with Language

Language Arts Standard: *Understands that reading progresses from left to right*

- Write the words to the following song on a chart. Include rebus pictures for the word *children*.

> **One little, two little, three little children,**
> **Four little, five little, six little children,**
> **Seven little, eight little, nine little children,**
> **Ten little children all in a row.**

- Point to the words, emphasizing left to right progression, as children sing the song to the tune of "Ten Little Indians."

- Invite ten children to sit in a row. Have them stand one by one as the song is sung until all ten are standing in a row.

Number Necklaces

Language Arts Standard: *Writes to produce numbers*

- Provide each child with ten two-inch circles and a piece of yarn about two feet long. Draw two small Xs on each circle about one inch apart to indicate where holes will be made for stringing on the necklace.

- Have children punch holes on the Xs on each circle using a hole punch. Younger children may need help using the hole punch.

- Invite children to write a number from 1 to 10 on each of the circles.

- Have them string the numbered circles on the yarn in numerical order.

- Tie the ends together and have children wear their necklaces.

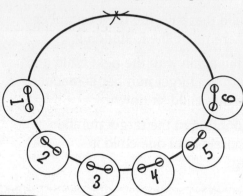

Edible Numbers

Art Standard: *Explores a variety of techniques to create original work*

- Mix together one-half cup of peanut butter, three tablespoons of powdered milk, and two tablespoons of honey for each child.

- Write two or three target numbers on a card for each child.

- Have children roll the dough into long ropes and use the dough to form the numbers on the card.

Caution: Be aware of children who may have food allergies.

Math Center

Math Standard:
Recognizes and names numbers

Magic Number Rubbings

- Make number cards by writing a number on a piece of cardboard with glue. Make the lines of glue thick. Allow the glue to dry so that it is clear.

- Provide children with thin newsprint paper, four clothespins, and crayons. Cut the paper to fit the size of the cardboard.

- Have children cover a number card with newsprint paper. Put a clothespin on each corner to hold the paper and card in place. Younger children may need help with the clothespins.

- Have children color the entire paper using back and forth strokes.

- Challenge children to name the number that is revealed.

Language Center

Language Arts Standard:
Recognizes rhyming words

Rhyming with Numbers

- Duplicate the sun, shoe, tree, door, and hive (p. 81). Color them, if desired. Glue the pictures to index cards and laminate them.

- Write the numbers from 1 to 5 on index cards.

- On the inside of a file folder, glue the number cards across the top. Glue blank cards below each number and laminate the folder.

- Invite children to match the picture card whose name rhymes with a number, such as *one* and *sun*. Have children place the correct picture card below each number.

123

Art Center

Art Standard:
Explores a variety of techniques to create original work

Sponge Painting Numbers

- Duplicate the numbers (p. 79 and p. 80) on construction paper. Cut them out.

- Set up a paint center with a desired color of tempera paint in a bowl and a clothespin attached to a small square sponge.

- Provide each child with a sheet of white construction paper and several number cutouts. Help children stick a small piece of double-sided tape on the back of each number cutout.

- Have children place the numbers on the construction paper in a pleasing arrangement so that none are overlapping.

- Invite children to dip the sponge into the paint. Then have them repeatedly dab the sponge onto the paper in order to cover the entire paper with paint.

- Have children remove the number cutouts to reveal white numbers.

Icky Bugs

- Read *The Icky Bug Counting Book* by Jerry Pallotta.

- Write the numbers 1 to 6 on 2-inch paper circles. Tape the circles in the cups of a muffin tin.

- Bury about 25 plastic insects in the sand table.

- Invite children to find the insects in the sand table. Then have them put the correct number of insects in each muffin tin cup, according to the number inside the cup.

Sensory Center

Math Standard:
Counts objects using one-to-one correspondence

Number Patterns

Use with "Numbers on Parade" on page 73, "Skip Counting" on page 74,
and "Sponge Painting Numbers" on page 78.

Numbers: Patterns
Sensational Seasons: Summer, SV 9781419033940

More Number Patterns
Use with "Numbers on Parade" on page 73, "Skip Counting" on page 74,
and "Sponge Painting Numbers" on page 78.

Numbers: Patterns
Sensational Seasons: Summer, SV 9781419033940

Picture Cards
Use with "Rhyming with Numbers" on page 77.

sun

shoe

tree

door

hive

Numbers: Patterns
Sensational Seasons: Summer, SV 9781419033940

Circus, Circus

Books to Read

A Color Clown Comes to Town by Jane Belk Moncure (Child's World)

Circus by Lois Ehlert (HarperCollins Juvenile Books)

Circus Caps for Sale by Esphyr Slobodkina (HarperTrophy)

Clifford at the Circus by Norman Bridwell (Cartwheel)

Emeline at the Circus by Marjorie Priceman (Dragonfly)

Last Night I Dreamed a Circus by Maya Gottfried (Knopf House Books for Young Readers)

Olivia Saves the Circus by Ian Falconer (Atheneum)

Paddington Bear at the Circus by Michael Bond (HarperCollins)

See the Circus (Lift the Flap Series) by H. A. Rey (Houghton Mifflin)

The Circus by Brian Wildsmith (Oxford University Press)

The Circus Alphabet by Linda Bronson (Henry Holt & Co.)

Circus Facts

Circuses began in ancient Rome and included lions, elephants, chariot races, and athletic performances on horses. The court jester was one of the first clowns. The jester often juggled, sang, and did routines to make the audience laugh. The circus, as we know it today, began with the exciting performances of a British cavalry soldier named Philip Astley around 1768. The traveling circus began in the United States in the early 1800s. The group would stop its wagons on the edge of town and pitch tents. Hackaliah Bailey put together a traveling circus that included an elephant. It was such a huge success that Bailey added other exotic animals to the show. Bailey partnered with P. T. Barnum, and then in 1907, their circus was sold to the Ringling Brothers.

Just Clowning Around

Materials

- blue craft paper
- border
- paper plates
- orange and white construction paper
- other bright-colored construction paper for hats
- bright-colored dot stickers
- small red balloons
- buttons
- markers
- cotton balls or pompoms
- bright tempera paints
- paintbrushes
- scissors
- stapler
- tape
- glue

Directions

Teacher Preparation: Cut equilateral triangles with nine-inch sides from construction paper. Blow up a balloon for each child to use as a clown nose. Tie a knot in each balloon. Provide a paper plate for each child. Poke a hole in the center of each paper plate and pull the knot on the balloon through to the back. Tape the knot in place. Cut a generous supply of orange paper strips. Cover the bulletin board with craft paper. Add a border and the caption. Staple clowns to the bulletin board.

1. Draw a mouth below the balloon nose on the paper plate. Then draw two "+" eyes above the nose. Glue a button in the center of each eye.

2. Glue a few orange strips for hair on each side of the face. Cut the strips to a desired length.

3. Decorate a triangle hat with dot stickers. Glue a cotton ball or pompom to the top of the hat. Glue the hat on the clown's head.

4. Paint children's hands. Have them make four handprints on white construction paper in an arc shape for a neck ruffle. Allow the paper to dry. Cut around the handprints and glue the ruffle along the bottom of the clown's face.

Tightrope Walkers

Language Arts Standard: *Begins to name letters of the alphabet*

- Discuss with children that tightrope walkers hold their arms out to their sides in order to help keep their balance as they walk across the high wire.

- Tape ten sheets of construction paper with short sides together on the floor. Tape the papers in a row to resemble a balance beam.

- Write a different letter of the alphabet on each sheet of paper. Write the letters so that they are all facing the same direction.

- Invite children to stand at one end of the paper row and lift their arms as tightrope walkers.

- Have children walk across the "high wire" from one end to the other. Have them name each letter as they step on it.

A Circus Story

Language Arts Standard: *Retells a story*

- Show children the cover of a circus story such as *Clifford at the Circus* by Norman Bridwell.

- Have them predict what they think the character on the cover will experience.

- Read the book to children.

- Invite children to retell the story. Encourage them to tell what happened at the beginning of the story, in the middle, and at the end.

Looking at Letters and Words

Language Arts Standard: *Recognizes rhyming words*

- Duplicate the rhyming picture cards (pp. 6–8). Mount them on construction paper and laminate them. Provide one card for each child.

- Have children name the pictures on the cards.

- Mix up the cards and scatter them on the floor or rug. Have children stand in a circle around the cards.

- Play some happy circus music and invite children to parade around the cards.

- Have children pick up a card when the music stops.

- Challenge children to find the person in the circle whose picture rhymes with their picture.

- Have partners name their rhyming pair.

Lion Tamers

Math Standard: *Uses concepts that include number recognition and counting*

- Cut and tape red streamers to the top of a large plastic hoop to make a ring of fire. Make number cards with the numbers 1 to 10.

- Hold the hoop and have children sit in a circle around it.

- Provide children with one lion headband like the one made in "Circus Lion Headbands" on page 88.

- Invite children to take turns putting on the headband, pretending to be a circus lion.

- Show children a number card to indicate how many times they are to jump through the ring of fire.

- Encourage all the children to count aloud each time the lion jumps through the hoop.

In Tune with Language

Language Arts Standard: *Begins to distinguish words in sentences*

- Write the words to the song below on sentence strips. Place the sentence strips in a pocket chart.

  I want to be a _____ **in the circus.**
  That is what I truly want to be.
  And if I was a _____ **in the circus,**
  Then everyone would cheer and clap for me!

- Make three word cards each for the words *clown, lion, acrobat, seal,* and *horse.* Insert two word cards for *clown* into the pocket chart on the blank lines.

- Invite children to learn the song above to the tune of "The Oscar Meyer Wiener Jingle."

- Show children the third word card for *clown.* Invite them to find the word *clown* in the song.

- Replace the *clown* word cards with the remaining cards to sing other verses. Have children find the words for each of the circus performers.

The Circus Is Coming to Town

Language Arts Standard: *Writes to communicate for a variety of purposes*

- Lead a discussion with children about how posters are used to tell people about a special happening or event.

- Show children samples of posters that use large print to tell about an event.

- Invite children to use crayons or markers to make colorful circus posters that announce the arrival of the circus.

- Write model poster texts on a chart for children to use as they make their own posters.

- Help them hang their posters on the wall around the classroom.

Circus Train Animals

Art Standard: *Explores a variety of techniques to create original work*

- Lead a discussion with children about the kinds of animals that are in a circus.

- Provide each child with a graham cracker and a few animal crackers on a paper plate. Tell children that they will be using the crackers to make a circus animal train car.

- Have children use a plastic knife to spread softened cream cheese on the graham cracker.

- Then have children place the animal crackers on the graham cracker.

- Invite children to squeeze thin lines of cake decorating icing from a tube to make the bars on their train car.

- Have children use a dab of cream cheese to attach two chocolate cookies for wheels on the car.

- Tell children to enjoy their circus train snack.

Caution: Be aware of children who may have food allergies.

**Circus: Writing Activity and Snack Idea**
Sensational Seasons: Summer, SV 9781419033940

Math Center

Math Standard:
Recognizes and names numbers

Clowning Around with Numbers

- Duplicate the activity master (p. 89) for each child.
- Write the numbers 0 to 10 on a sentence strip. Place it on a table with 11 plastic milk caps.
- Challenge children to find the numbers from 0 to 10 on the activity master and color them red.
- As children color each number, have them cover the corresponding number on the sentence strip with a milk cap and name the number.
- Invite children to color the picture using crayons or markers.

Language Center

Language Arts Standard:
Identifies letters in own name

Balancing Names

- Duplicate a seal (p. 90) for each child.
- Cut out a generous supply of two-inch circles to be used as balls.
- Provide each child with a sheet of construction paper, a seal, and a ball for each letter in his or her name.
- Invite children to color the seal and glue it at the bottom of the construction paper.
- Have them write each letter in their name on a separate ball. Younger children may need help.
- Starting at the seal's nose, have children balance the balls in the correct order to spell their name. Glue the balls in place.

Sensational Seasons: Summer, SV 9781419033940

Art Center

*Language Arts
Standard:*
*Organizes writing from
left to right*

Circus Lion Headbands

- Cut a 2-inch by 18-inch strip of yellow construction paper for each child. Also cut a few extras.
- Cut a generous supply of 2-inch by 9-inch strips of brown construction paper.
- Adjust the yellow strip to fit each child's head and staple the strip to form a headband. Use the extra strips to extend the length if necessary.
- Help children fold the brown strips in accordion pleats for the lion's mane.
- Have children glue the ends of the strips around the sides and back of the headband.
- Have children write the word *lion* across the front of the headband.

- Paint the tip of children's noses and paint whiskers on their cheeks using black face paint or watercolors.
- Invite children to wear their "mane" and pretend to be a circus lion.

Science Center

Science Standard:
*Begins to understand
about scientific
inquiry*

Circus Forces

- Duplicate the picture cards (p. 90). Mount them on index cards and write the labels *push* and *pull*.
- Display push toys such as a lawnmower, a car, and a shovel. Also display some pull toys such as a wagon, a duck on a string, and a rake.
- Discuss with children how a push or a pull is needed to make each toy move. Explain that a force is a push or a pull, and a force is needed to make things move.
- Lead children in a discussion of circus activities that show a push or a pull force.
- Place the labeled index cards on the floor or on a table. Invite children to sort the push and pull toys and put them under the correct cards.

Sensational Seasons: Summer, SV 9781419033940

Name _____

Circus

Directions: Use with "Clowning Around with Numbers" on page 87. Have children find and color the numbers from 0 to 10 using a red crayon. Then invite them to color the picture.

Circus: Activity Master
Sensational Seasons: Summer, SV 9781419033940

Seal Pattern
Use with "Balancing Names" on page 87.

seal

Push or Pull Picture Cards
Use with "Circus Forces" on page 88.

Assessment

We observe children every day in our classrooms. Most of the time, these observations are done on an informal basis. We may not even realize the valuable information we gain from them. Often we recognize how much we really do know about the children in our classroom when we formally assess them.

Our observations are only the very beginning of assessment in our classrooms. The terms **assessment** and **evaluation** are often used interchangeably, yet assessment must occur before evaluation can take place. To assess means to collect data. To evaluate means to analyze that data.

During our daily observations, we collect data on each of the children in our classrooms. However, to make that assessment worthwhile, it is important to go one step further and evaluate the data that we collect. The key to assessment in our classrooms is the evaluations we make and how we use those evaluations to inform instruction. We cannot just assess children. Without evaluation, the assessment is hardly worth noting.

Just as we create lesson plans for each day, so must we plan assessment opportunities. Assessment does not just happen. In addition, we must plan time for evaluation of the data we collect.

On the following pages, you will find some valuable assessments for your preschoolers.

Anecdotal Records

An anecdotal record is a record of the behaviors a child exhibits during the day. It tells a story about what the child can do. Over time, anecdotal records create snapshots of the children in your class. Anecdotal records are probably one of the easiest assessment tools to use in your classroom. This tool is an appropriate one to use on a daily basis, and the time devoted to taking anecdotal records is very minimal.

Tips for Taking Anecdotal Records

- Keep your anecdotal record system close at hand. This will allow you to note behaviors quickly.

- Be sure to date your records.

- Set goals for the number of anecdotal records you will make each day. For instance, every day of the week you may want to make notes on one-fifth of your children.

- It may be helpful to choose a focus for your anecdotal records each day. This may be particularly helpful if you are just beginning to use anecdotal records in your classroom. For example, one week you may want to note what kinds of writing each child is engaged in during writing activities.

- Attempt to keep your anecdotal records positive. Rather than noting what a child **can't** do, note what he or she **can** do instead. For example, *Today Mary was able to navigate a return sweep while reading her guided reading book.* Don't worry about the fact that the child wasn't able to match the written words entirely with the spoken words. Keep the focus on what children can do. You will then find your instruction also remains positive.

Sensational Seasons: Summer, SV 9781419033940

- Set aside time at least once a month to review and evaluate your anecdotal records. Note any patterns you find within a group of students or a pattern you see emerging with one particular child.

- Use your anecdotal records to inform your instruction. For instance, if you find a group of children who are continually attempting to write poetry during writing time, you may want to pull them together to talk about various types of poetry writing. If you note a group of children who are having difficulty retelling stories they have read, pull them together in a group to work on retelling simple stories. These examples illustrate the use of anecdotal records to inform your instruction.

Organizing Anecdotal Records

The following is just one organizational system that can help to make your use of anecdotal records efficient. Write each child's name at the bottom of a 4″ x 6″ ruled index card. Then lay the index cards on a clipboard in a layered effect. Attach the cards with tape.

As you plan your assessment opportunities, keep the clipboard and a pen—which can be attached to the clipboard with a string—with you. Note behaviors you observe on a child's index card. Be sure to date your observations. Plan to note behaviors for at least one-fifth of the children in your class each day. That will allow you to have at least one anecdotal record for each child each week.

As you fill index cards, replace them. File the completed cards in your children's portfolios.

Anecdotal records can be taken for any subject. Be sure not only to date your anecdotal records, but to record the subject matter so you can quickly look through the records and find patterns in a particular subject. Once a month, spend five to ten minutes rereading the anecdotal records on one child. Look for patterns to address in your instruction.

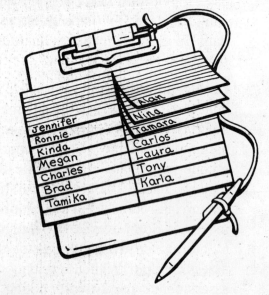

Assessment
Sensational Seasons: Summer, SV 9781419033940

ABC/Phonemic Awareness Assessment

To assess children's alphabet knowledge, copy the ABC assessment card on page 94. Laminate it for durability. Also make copies of the ABC assessment recording sheet on this page. Plan to assess children on their alphabet knowledge a minimum of twice a year, once at the beginning and once at the end.

Teacher Directions:

- As you call a child over to work with you, show him or her the ABC assessment card. Say to the child: *What are these?* Do not use the word "letters," as you will want to note what the child calls these symbols.
- Show only one row of letters at a time. This will allow children to focus better.
- Point to each letter and say: *Tell me what this is.* The child should tell you the name of the letter. Record the child's response.
- You can also use these blackline masters to assess phonemic awareness. Simply point to each letter and say: *Tell me what sound this letter makes.*

Child's Name: _____ Date: _____

Child's Approximate Age: _____ Child's Score: _____ /54

Ask: *What are these?* Child's response: _____

✔ = correct response   x = incorrect response   O = no response

a ____	e ____	i ____	m ____	q ____	u ____	y ____
b ____	f ____	j ____	n ____	r ____	v ____	z ____
c ____	g ____	k ____	o ____	s ____	w ____	a ____
d ____	h ____	l ____	p ____	t ____	x ____	g ____
A ____	E ____	I ____	M ____	Q ____	U ____	Y ____
B ____	F ____	J ____	N ____	R ____	V ____	Z ____
C ____	G ____	K ____	O ____	S ____	W ____	
D ____	H ____	L ____	P ____	T ____	X ____	

Assessment
Sensational Seasons: Summer, SV 9781419033940

ABC Assessment Card

a e i m q u y

b f j n r v z

c g k o s w a

d h l p t x g

··

A E I M Q U Y

B F J N R V Z

C G K O S W

D H L P T X

Assessment
Sensational Seasons: Summer, SV 9781419033940

Emergent Reading Checklist

Teacher Directions:

During whole-group, small-group, or independent reading time, observe children as they are engaged in the reading process. Be sure to note a child's reading behavior at least once each quarter during the year. This checklist can also be useful at report card time.

Name: _____ Grade: _____

	Date of Entries			✔
Enjoys listening to books				
Confidently participates in shared reading				
Makes meaningful predictions using the story and pictures as clues				
Retells stories and rhymes				
Approximates book language				
Uses pictures to comprehend text				
Realizes that print carries a message				
Demonstrates book handling skills				
Locates the name of the author and illustrator				
Recognizes parts of a book (cover, title, title page)				
Demonstrates directionality: left to right				
Demonstrates directionality: top to bottom				
Identifies uppercase and lowercase letters				
Demonstrates an understanding of letters and words				
Identifies some sounds				
Matches spoken words to print				
Recognizes own name and common environmental print				
Reads some one-syllable and high-frequency words				
Chooses to look at/read books from a variety of sources				
Can sit still for short periods of time to read a book				

Checklist
Sensational Seasons: Summer, SV 9781419033940

Emergent Writing Checklist

Teacher Directions:

Observe children during whole-group writing experiences and independent writing experiences. Be sure to note student writing behavior at least once each quarter during the year. This checklist can also be useful at report card time.

Name: _____ Grade: _____

	Date of Entries			✔
Makes pre-letter writing marks on paper				
Writes letters, symbols, or numerals randomly				
Writes some uppercase and lowercase letters of the alphabet				
Demonstrates directionality of letters				
Writes initial consonants				
Writes partially phonetically spelled words				
Writes some completely phonetically spelled words				
Writes high-frequency words randomly				
Writes a few known words correctly				
Uses random finger pointing when reading his or her writing				

Checklist
Sensational Seasons: Summer, SV 9781419033940